An Inland See

A brief History of
the Roman Catholic
Diocese of Burlington

By Howard Coffin

Printed in the United States of America
ISBN: 0-9711192-0-1
Printed by L. Brown and Sons Printing Inc., Barre, Vermont

Two eras of Burlington Catholic history appear in this photo taken about 1866. The Cathedral is under construction. The church in front of the Cathedral is Father O'Callaghan's 1841 St. Mary's on the southeast corner of St. Paul and Cherry Streets.

Writer's Note

IN THE SUMMER OF 1998, Msgr. John McSweeney, a lover of Vermont history, approached me about the possibility of writing a popular history of the Catholic Church in Vermont. I told him that while the subject interested me, I had only a brief window of time available. He said it was the hope of Bishop Kenneth Angell to bring a book out for the Millennium, thus only very little time was, indeed, available for writing. After visiting the Diocese of Burlington's archive and seeing its resources, and having known one of its archivists, David Blow, I was confident the archive would be a ready source of information and assistance. I then met archivist William Goss, who proved to be a veritable encyclopedia of Church history. These two capable historians were, at the time, in the process of writing a lengthy and detailed history of the Catholic faith in Vermont. They made their unfinished work available to me, without which I could not have written this book. The history of the Diocese of Burlington is rich and deep and is an important, untold part of Vermont's history. It is a story that particularly needs to be set down as we enter a new millennium, for human beings too often tend to look only ahead, and the intriguing story of Catholicism in Vermont is far too important to be lost.

Sadly, as this book neared completion, Bill Goss died rather suddenly. This book could not have been written without a great deal of patient assistance, particularly from Bill and David Blow, and from Msgr. John McSweeney. Also making important contributions were Bishop Louis Gelineau, Bishop Angell, Father Wendell Searles, Father Walter Miller, Msgr. Edward Gelineau, Msgr. Francis Flanagan, the late Msgr. Edwin Buckley and the late Father Omer Dufault, Prof. Vincent Naramore, and the many other Catholics throughout the state who patiently answered my questions and participated in the group history discussions so kindly arranged by local parish priests. The estimable Vermont historian T. D. Seymour Bassett was of much help, as he has been on all books I have written, and kindly made his files on the Catholic Church in Vermont available.

As a child who grew up a Protestant in Vermont, I had many Catholic friends. After all, Woodstock has long had a sizable and active Catholic parish. In my early years, a next door neighbor, Miss Ada Mary Maynes, who like my mother was a switchboard operator for the local telephone company, told me things about her religion. She was a devout Catholic, the product of an Irish family that had fled the potato famines, settled for a time on Prince Edward Island, then had come south to make a home in Vermont. Aunt Ada, as I called her, a loving and good-natured "honorary aunt," was always cautious in talking about Catholicism, for she believed religion was a matter for me and my parents to discuss. But in our conversations she instilled in me a deep curiosity about, and respect for, her church. At long last, I feel I really know something about what took her on foot day after day, a mile round trip, no matter the weather, to Mass at Our Lady of the Snows Church on South Street.

I hope this book is interesting and readable, and will inspire curiosity about the history of Catholicism in Vermont. May it be a stepping stone to that complete history which is so much needed. I would like to dedicate my efforts in writing *An Inland See* to one of the dearest people I have met along the road of life, my Aunt Ada, whose earthly remains rest on a green hillside in Woodstock, her days of this world, always filled with kindness, long done. With such quietly remarkable human beings are our childhoods, if we look back on them with a sense of love and wonder, peopled. She was truly special and she was, above all else, devoutly Catholic.

Without archives, history could not be written. Without the wonderful archive of the Diocese of Burlington that Bill Goss did so much to create, this book would not have been possible.

Howard Coffin

Introduction to Diocesan History

It is the duty of Catholics who live today to record, preserve and pass on our story to those yet to come. This duty is entrusted to us from our Church's very first historical archivists, Matthew, Mark, Luke and John.

In this Great Jubilee Year of the Lord, 2000, we celebrate the Beginning of Christian History with the Birth of our Savior, Jesus Christ. Thanks to St. Luke, we have a beautiful account of God's most gracious gift to humanity. And then it was Matthew, some 30 years later, who recorded the birth of our Lord's church. St. Matthew tells us that Jesus was in the town of Caesaria Philippi, when He proclaimed to Peter, the Fisherman:

> **"You are 'Rock', and upon this rock I will build my Church,**
> **and the jaws of death will not prevail against it."**
> **(Matthew 16:18)**

And a journey of 20 Christian Centuries began.

It would be some 1600 years before the Catholic Church arrived in Vermont. Samuel de Champlain, a Catholic explorer, became the first white man to sail up Lake Champlain in 1609. Some 50 years later, the Jesuits established several missions along our beautiful lake. The Bishops of Baltimore and Quebec looked after the spiritual interests of early Catholic settlers and Native Americans until Burlington became part of the newly erected Diocese of Boston in 1808. Then, in 1830, the 14th state received its first resident priest when Bishop Fenwick of Boston sent in the energetic Reverend Jeremiah O'Callaghan. Under Father O'Callaghan's guidance, Vermont grew to five priests, ten churches and some 20,000 Catholics by 1853 when the Holy See declared the state a diocese, with Burlington as its see.

The Most Reverend Louis Joseph Mary Theodore de Goesbriand was elected to lead and serve the new Diocese by Pope Pius IX. The Bishop's motto was "Deus Providebit"..."God Will Provide." It indicates how profoundly Vermont's first shepherd relied on the historical and biblical recordings of our early church for encouragement and faith in proclaiming the

Good News against considerable challenges and obstacles. When all else fails, turn it over to God.

Almost 150 years and eight bishops later, we are still trusting that "God Will Provide" as we face our own new, yet strangely ancient, challenges and obstacles. And now I, as bishop, face these tests with a new motto in mind: "To Serve the Lord with Gladness." We can do so, because we have the Word and the encouragement of how those before us struggled to proclaim that Word. We know that because they have lovingly and carefully preserved their story for us. We now do likewise, adding our own moments in history and passing them along so that you who follow will continue to preserve his Word and help His Church to prevail until the end of time. In this endeavor, we are especially indebted to Monsignor John R. McSweeney, archivists: David Blow and the late William Goss; and author Howard Coffin.

I pray that "God Will Provide" you with the courage and the grace to "Serve the Lord with Gladness."

+ Kenneth A. Angell

Most Reverend Kenneth A. Angell
Eighth Bishop of Burlington

Table of Contents

1

IN THE SOFT LIGHT of an early-August morning in Vermont, the man destined to become the spiritual leader of all the world's Roman Catholics placed a folding card table beneath the branches of a plum tree in the back pasture of a Pomfret farmhouse. Wearing vestments borrowed from Our Lady of the Snows Church in nearby Woodstock, Karol Cardinal Wojtyla, who in a little more than two years would become Pope John Paul II, said Mass as several friends, and a donkey, goat, and pony looked on.

"He loved it here," said Anna-Teresa Houthakker, who with her husband, Hendrik, hosted the cardinal on their 200-year-old Pomfret farm. It was late July 1976 when Wojtyla first came to Vermont after lecturing at Harvard

Hendrik S. Houthakker and Anna-Teresa Tymieniecka
at the inauguration of the monument under the plum tree — 1984.

University. The visit to America had been an important one for the cardinal of Krakow. His recognition factor among Americans had risen considerably by his delivery of an important address at America's most prestigious university. And he had been introduced at a university luncheon by his friend Hendrik, an event attended by many members of the Harvard faculty and representatives of the press, as "the next pope." The Houthakkers tell of Cardinal Wojtyla's Vermont days—how he swam in a neighbor's farm pond, pitched hay, and walked the steep hills that overlook the valley of the White River. They recall that the cardinal said Mass very early each day so that their son could be present before his 10 mile morning bicycle ride to his job in Woodstock. And they talk of the cardinal sitting on a fallen tree at the edge of the lawn saying morning prayers.

"He said that a mountainous area he particularly loved in southern Poland was like this part of Vermont," Hendrik Houthakker recalled in 1998. "He stayed with us three days and then happily accepted an invitation to spend a short vacation at the end of August." Photographs of Wojtyla in Pomfret show him looking relaxed, happy, and vigorous, sometimes wearing a plaid shirt.

The hills of Pomfret rise steep and tree covered from the narrow valleys of splashing brooks that feed the White River, a winding deep-pooled course that on days of clouds or in moonlight can appear as white as its name. To stand far above the valley on the ledgy summits of the Pomfret hills is to see line upon line of Vermont ridges marching west toward the Green Mountains or east toward the White Mountains of New Hampshire. The valley floors, where land has been cleared and homes erected, are so abruptly far below that they can hardly be seen at all. It was to those heights that Cardinal Wojtyla took himself on several locust-song days of late summer in the bicentennial year of America. There are few places more beautiful in all Vermont.

The scenes presented from those high hills are of a land that seems to have been little changed by the hand of man. Indeed, from such hilltops, the landscape must look much as it would have to the Native Americans who for so long lived in deep harmony with the land that would one day become Vermont. So it must also have appeared to the first people of European descent who wended their cautious way into the mysterious and jumbled landscape of the north country. So far as is known, the first European to look upon any part of the Vermont landscape was, of course, a French explorer who made his way nearly four centuries ago up the long bright lake that would eventually bear his name. Samuel de Champlain, a French sea captain and the son of a sea captain—along with two fellow explorers whose names have been lost to history— opened the door to Catholicism in Vermont.

In the early summer of 1609, Champlain and his party, after a cruel winter spent along the St. Lawrence River in a new settlement called Quebec, set out southward in canoes guided by a party of Algonquin. In early July, they emerged against the steady current of the Richelieu River into a long inland sea. Champlain's Indian guides told him that the great lake extended to the east almost to the mountains, where there were "beautiful valleys and other stretches fertile in grain." At one point in his exploration of the long lake, Champlain stopped at a place where a great grove of chestnut trees grew. As the historian Ralph Nading Hill later noted, at only one place has it ever been determined that such trees grew along the lake—near the mouth of the Winooski River. Thus Champlain may well have set foot at Burlington, where the Diocese of Burlington would one day be headquartered. Though the author of a centenary history of the diocese noted in 1953 that Champlain may not have been born to the Catholic faith, he also quoted another scholar: "Champlain's thought and action was dedicated to one end, 'to the foundation in America of a great kingdom, to be ruled with justice and mercy, by France, but for God.' "

Though the French were not swift to seize on Champlain's discoveries for purposes of empire, soon to the Champlain Valley came the "Black Robes," Jesuit priests intent on bringing their faith to the peoples of the new lands. Nearly three-and-a-half centuries later, a filmmaker would produce a motion picture based on their adventures, *Black Robes*. The film concerns a young priest, fresh in the New World from France, who ventured into the American wilds intent on bringing Christianity to the Indians. In a remark-

Site of Fort St. Anne, Isle La Motte, built in 1666. The first Mass in Vermont was celebrated here that year. It is now the site of St. Anne's Shrine.

able early scene, the priest walks alone into the forest one winter morning and briefly becomes lost. While seeking his way, he looks up at the great overarching trees of a virgin forest and for a moment sees them transformed into the soaring vaults of a Gothic cathedral. Such visions may have guided some early missionaries, though the reality of the new lands was often to prove cruelly harsh. According to legend, St. Isaac Jogues, perhaps the most famous of the Black Robes, while a prisoner of the Iroquois, may have been tortured on Isle La Motte. Maimed by his captors, he returned to Europe but was soon back in the New World as a missionary. There he would again become a prisoner and die at the hands of his torturers.

In 1666, Pierre de St. Paul, with the title of Sieur de la Motte, was sent with 300 men by the French government to build and garrison a fort on an island that took his name, the fourth in a chain of bastions extending along the Richelieu River and into Champlain. The just-completed fort was, on July 26, 1666, dedicated to St. Anne—it being her feast day. A Mass was celebrated, probably by regimental chaplain Father DuBois, and a salvo of muskets was fired.

Jesuit missionaries built a stone chapel near the mouth of the Missisquoi in 1700 close to present-day Swanton. By that time, the French presence in the Champlain Valley extended 75 miles south to strategic Chimney Point, where a small settlement was established. Close by, across the lake narrows at Crown Point on the western shore, construction of a stone fortress was completed by 1734. Limestone Fort St. Frederick, walled and with a castlelike keep rising four stories above the lakeshore, had much the appearance of a fortified European castle. A Swedish traveler, Peter Kalm, visited the fort in 1749 and noted, "On the eastern part of the fort is a high tower, which is proof against bomb shells, provided with very thick and substantial walls, and well stored with cannon from the bottom almost to the very top: the governor lives in the tower. In the terre plein of the fort is a well built little church, and houses of stone for the officers and soldiers." The fort was blown up by the retreating French upon the northward advance of British forces under Lord Jeffrey Amherst in 1759. But the bastion's stone foundations still lie beside the lake, and within the old walls, a sign identifies the location of the tiny chapel that served not only soldiers, but also settlers from the far side of the lake.

The French and Indian Wars came to the Champlain Valley as Britain and France struggled for control of North America through more than three decades of intermittent warfare. Territorial disputes followed along the border of New York and the New Hampshire Grants, which became Vermont. Then came the American Revolution, full-fledged warfare between rebellious colonists and the English armies, aggravated by the seizing of Fort Ticonderoga by Ethan Allen's Green Mountain Boys. Two important British military campaigns swept down Champlain—the latter in 1777 ending with the decisive conflict of the war, the American victory at Saratoga. Though Vermonters had fought well in the independence struggle, their attempts to gain admission to the new United States would be thwarted for 14 years. Thus Vermont existed as a republic, a small and independent nation, until becoming a state in 1791.

There is little historical record of Catholicism in Vermont during those decades. One story, however, concerns a famous conversion—that of the daughter of the fiery Ethan Allen, a deist who held with no organized religion. Yet his daughter, Fanny Allen, convinced her mother and stepfather to allow her to visit Montreal and study the French language in a convent there. On a fall day in 1808, Fanny Allen became a novice of the Religious Hospitalers of St. Joseph. Fanny claimed that an event from her childhood was instrumental in her conversion. She said that one day, while living in Sunderland in southwestern Vermont, she was upon the bank of a river (surely the Battenkill) when a frightening beast arose out of its waters. At that moment there appeared beside her an aged man, who told her to flee immediately. Many years later, while in Montreal, the young lady saw behind the altar of a church a painting of the Holy Family. She recognized in the portrait of St. Joseph the face of the man who had come to her aid years before.

Rev. Pierre Marie Mignault of Chambly, Quebec, ministered to the Catholic population of the northern Champlain Valley 1818–54. His statue is in Chambly.

Most settlers were entering Vermont from southern New England, and most were Protestants. But a few Catholics were filtering in, primarily from Canada, to settle in northern Vermont. Also, a few descendants of French settlers had held on in Vermont from the days of the French empire. Soon after his installation as bishop of Quebec in 1806, Joseph-Octave Plessis wrote of "the portion of the state of Vermont nearest our boundary, where I hear there are many Canadians and others destitute of spiritual aid." But it was not until 1815 that Catholics in Vermont gained any official recognition from the church hierarchy. In 1810, the Diocese of Boston was created, and in 1815 the bishop of Boston, Jean de Cheverus, dispatched Fr. François Matignon on a journey from Boston to Three Rivers, Quebec. The priest took a circuitous route via Whitehall, New York, then up Lake Champlain. En route, a Protestant woman told him of the presence of some 100 Catholics in the Burlington area. Father Matignon stopped by on his return trip and on October 15, 1815, records of the Boston Cathedral Show, he baptized 18 children.

The number of Catholics in Vermont steadily, though slowly, increased, primarily due to Irish immigration. In 1819, Bishop Plessis of Quebec sent Fr. Pierre Mignault south into Vermont to do missionary work along Lake Champlain. His visits continued until 1853. Other priests ventured into Vermont visiting small Catholic colonies of a few families each in Castleton, Wallingford, Tinmouth, Bennington, Shrewsbury, Poultney, Dorset, Middlebury, and Pittsford. To the north, Catholic groups of growing size were located not only at Burlington, but at Swanton, St. Albans, and Fairfield. At least twice in the early 1820s, Bishop Cheverus came to the state. Other priests from time to time made their way to the north country, but apparently stayed only briefly.

Then on July 6, 1830, at the behest of Bp. Benedict Fenwick of Boston, Rev. Jeremiah O'Callaghan, a native of Ireland, arrived in Vermont. Father O'Callaghan was a firebrand—having developed in Europe a reputation as a harsh and outspoken critic of banks and most lenders of money. Indeed, he had written books on usury. In one, he said of his native Ireland, "How do the millions live, who have neither means to lend, nor credit to borrow; or how will the several millions of the widows and orphans, and gentlemen, now live, who are reduced to beggary by the pressure of the national debt, the usury of the fundholders, the usury and failure of the banks of England and Ireland?" Clearly, he was a man who spoke his mind. He wrote upon his arrival in Vermont:

> Catholics, principally Irish immigrants were as sheep without shepherds, scattered through the woods and villages, amidst the wolves in sheep's clothing—amidst fanatics of all creeds, or rather of no creed; all enticing them by bribery and menaces to protracted meetings, camp meetings, Sun-

day Schools and so forth. As I was the very first Catholic pastor sent to them, their joy seemed to know no bounds on my arrival. There were eight congregations, varying from 10 to 100 (in number), from 20 to 30 miles asunder. I was hardly able to visit them all in two months.

Bishop Fenwick's first instructions to O'Callaghan were, in the priest's words, "to visit successively Wallingford, Pittsford, Vergennes, and Burlington, with such other places in their neighborhood as may have Catholics abiding in them." O'Callaghan wrote:

> I made a beginning in the house of Mr. James Sherlock, Wallingford, a religious man, and fearing God with all his house, and praying always; who was, I think, a native of County of Wexford, Ireland, and emigrated soon after to Michigan. Our little congregation consisted of six families only, who were in famine, not a famine of bread and thirst and water, but of hearing the word of the Lord. I drew their attention to the vanity of the world, to the eternal glory that is promised to those who suffer for justice's sake, to the fidelity of our fathers who preserved and handed down to us the sacred deposit which they had received, through the holy apostle Patrick, from the successor of St. Peter, and to the necessity of loving and keeping his commandments, that the Father, and the Son, and the Holy Ghost might come and dwell with us. I offered up the holy sacrifice for the living and the dead, admitted to the communion of the altar all the adults, and baptized three infants. From that grain of mustard-seed had grown up a large tree, a numerous and respectable congregation, in the surrounding country.

The articulate O'Callaghan was most pleasantly surprised to receive, upon arrival in Burlington, an offer from Col. Archibald Hyde —a Protestant later to convert to Catholicism— of five acres on the northern outskirts of the town for the location of a church. On September 9, 1832, a small wooden edifice, St. Mary's, the first Catholic church in Vermont, was dedicated. Bishop Fenwick came from Boston to see the new church and described it as "situated on a beautiful eminence close by the town." He also noted, "There is a gallery for singers. Everything in fact, about the church, is extremely neat. It is likewise ornamented with a small Gothick steeple." Of the dedicatory service, Fenwick wrote, "It was fortunate that there were in Burlington a number of French Canadians who had a few years before emigrated to this country. Among them were three or four tolerably well versed in the plain-chant, who could go through the service. These formed the choir and their voices were far from being bad. During the Mass several French canticles were sung which added much to the service."

In 1834, likely at the little church, a funeral was held for a young girl who had drowned on the Burlington waterfront. Father O'Callaghan presided, and a University of Vermont student, obviously a Protestant, was among those in attendance. The student told of it to a friend, who wrote: "The old priest prayed earnestly for the deliverance of the soul from purgatory. Coming away he (the student) asked a woman if she supposed his praying for the soul would do any good. 'Yes, yes,' said she. 'Oh you are a blue skin, blue skin.' Then about a dozen Irish men started up around him and ordered him to be silent. 'Go to the priest,' they say, 'he can tell you what good it does. We know nothing about it, nor do you either.'"

St. Mary's Church stood only five years, destroyed by a fire of suspicious origin in 1838. O'Callaghan wrote to Bishop Fenwick on May 12 of that year, "I am sorry to inform you that our church here was reduced to ashes by the

Middlebury church erected by Rev. John Daly 1839–40 and replaced by the present church in 1895.

incendiary Tuesday night last; no particle of the edifice, or of the contents is saved, except your chalice and patina that were usually carried into the house." The site of Vermont's first Catholic church today is part of the large St. Joseph's Cemetery in Burlington's North End, which is the outgrowth of the little church's burying ground. Where the historic building once was located, headstones stand above the mortal remains of Murphys and McCabes, Ryans and Kelleys, Hartigans, O'Briens, and Caseys.

Father O'Callaghan wrote of a visit in 1841 to

Former church in Castleton, the oldest surviving one in the state.

the congregation in St. Albans, where a public building was used for a church: "The court house was crowded at an early hour. The service commenced at 10 o'clock . . . I preached on the subject of Confirmation to a crowded audience; and as many of those who were present did not understand English, I also addressed them in French about half an hour. After which I gave Confirmation to individuals. The Court House was far too small for the immense crowd."

Not all visits were so successful, as O'Callaghan admitted in a letter to Bishop Fenwick in the winter of 1842:

> On my last visit to Vergennes, an Irish Catholic girl came with an English Protestant, a laborer of one arm, to get married. He knew not one word of the Lord's Prayer, nor of the Creed, nor of the Unity, Trinity of God, nor the Commandments, nor any one particle of the Christian religion. The disparity of religion, in addition to the loss of his one arm, showed me the unfitness of the match. Consequently I argued with them both, face to face, against their intention, telling them that each would do well to chose a spouse of his or her religious way of thinking, but I laboured in vain. She presently said in the presence of the company: "If you will not marry us, another clergyman will." Away they went at once, accompanied by several Irish boys and girls, and were married by a Squire.

Father O'Callaghan's baptismal record, the oldest Catholic record extant in Vermont, survives in the diocesan archive in Burlington. In it, scribed in O'Callaghan's determined hand, are the names and dates of baptisms throughout Vermont. It can fairly be said that O'Callaghan probably knew personally every Catholic living in Vermont in his time. In 1837, sent to Vermont by Bishop Fenwick to assist O'Callaghan came an Irish Franciscan, Rev. John B. Daly. Father Daly's tireless work strengthened, or created, Catholicism in such communities as Rutland, Pittsford, Norwich, Windsor, Manchester, and Bennington.

In Burlington, St. Mary's Church, in the downtown, a brick building located at the corner of St. Paul and Cherry Streets, was rebuilt and dedicated in 1841. Ten years later on high ground near the original St. Mary's, St. Joseph's was dedicated, church of the first French-speaking parish in New England. By then the potato famines and the coming of the railroads had brought a steady Irish migration to Vermont, and the number of Catholics in the state was dramatically on the rise. Also on the rise, among the Yankee population, was anti-Catholic sentiment. It showed through when the ever-outspoken Father O'Callaghan criticized Rev. John Wheeler, president of the University of Vermont, for talking politics. A local paper responded,

> This reverend Paddy . . . according to his own showing, has thrice been spewed from the church and his native country as a scatter-brained disorganizer. That such an individual should find our religion, our laws, our institutions, and the whole framework of society wrong, is certainly not wonderful; and that he should content himself with simply denouncing our businessmen as cut-throats, our clergy as imposters, and our statesmen and legislators as bribed and venal orators, indicates a degree of modest charity.

By 1852, at least 10 churches stood in Vermont, including St. Patrick's in Fairfield, St. Louis in Highgate, St. Mary's in Swanton, Our Lady of Good Help in Brandon, St. John the Baptist in Castleton, and Burlington's St. Mary's and St. Joseph's. And there was a little church on Montpelier's Court Street, located in an old courthouse purchased by local Catholics as a house of worship. A legislator, and recent convert, Sen. Dewitt Clinton Clarke, wrote to his wife on November 3, 1850, about the little church:

> I attended Mass . . . stealing quietly away from my seat in the Senate Chamber. Mass was celebrated in the new church, within a dozen rods of the State House. The interior is wholly

unfinished, but it did seem to me like worshipping God "in his Holy Temple."

The little building would serve as Montpelier's Catholic church for nine years. A new church, St. Augustine's— an imposing two-towered structure— would replace it in 1859, built almost beside the State House in as brash a statement of Catholic pride as Vermont has ever seen.

By 1852, there were perhaps 20,000 of the faith within the state, served by five priests. Such were the numbers that the First Plenary Council of Baltimore decided, in 1853, that Vermonters deserved a Catholic bishop of their own. The Diocese of Burlington was formally created by papal brief on July 29, 1853. All the while, Father O'Callaghan not only continued energetically serving his Vermont parishioners, but had also taken the faith to northern New Hampshire. He was the first priest to say Mass in many Vermont towns, including Waterbury, Enosburg, and Fairfield. And he continued his writing, which never lost its fire. In 1852, he published a book titled *Atheism of Brownson's Reviews: Unity and Trinity of God; Divinity and Humanity of Jesus Christ; Banks and Paper Money,* deploring in it the "terrific deluge of infidelity rushing down in these latter days upon all humanity." Moving to Massachusetts in 1854, O'Callaghan remained active as a priest for several more years, also continuing to write, never losing his outspokenness. Late in life, he looked back on his childhood in Ireland, in another century, and wrote of his parents:

They taught me to love God above all things, and to shudder at any, even the smallest violation of His law; to love our neighbor for God's sake, and never to turn our face from the poor man. And, I see, when nearly all the family have embarked into eter-

"Mass Rock," Moretown.

IN MEMORY OF
REV. FATHER O'CALLAGHAN
WHO SAID MASS ON THIS
STONE IN 1853

nity, and when the world with her deceitful allurements is fast receding from myself, that my parents' was the best legacy that could be made.

The old priest, the first resident Catholic pastor of Vermont, died in Holyoke, Massachusetts, in 1861, the year the Civil War began. Having been born during the American Revolution, Father O'Callaghan expired at 81. Bishop Fitzpatrick of Massachusetts entered the following thoughts on the departed priest in his diary on February 23, 1861:

> He was an eccentric and somewhat noted character, having printed and . . . circulated several books on the subject of usury, banking, pew-leasing in other churches, graveyards etc., etc. . . . He was a man of fair natural talent, slender education, limited knowledge and indomitable spirit as well as great presumption . . . He was very fond of attacking any letters, pastorals, or writings by bishops or archbishops and always thought he could observe in them heresies or infidelity. Many prelates in the United States have received from him denunciatory letters of this kind. But no one heeded him and he was considered crazy. In fact he was . . . He was for over 30 years a missionary in New England and labored most of the time in Vermont, where the Catholics, being poor, gave him no chance to enforce his queer notions on what he called usury. He was faithful as a priest, indefatigable as a worker . . .

It would seem that the general memory of O'Callaghan— particularly among Catholics in the little backcountry towns of the Green Mountains, where his untiring visits represented the only show of the cloth to many newly-arrived from far away— would have been commented on far more kindly than by Bishop Fitzpatrick. Indeed, there stands today, on a large flat rock in an old cow pasture in the central Vermont town of Moretown, a monument to Father O'Callaghan. The small granite marker notes that on that spot in 1853, Father O'Callaghan said Mass. Well before they had a church, Catholics of the Mad River Valley had gathered in an upland pasture to hear the words of Vermont's great pioneer Catholic. By the time O'Callaghan died, Catholicism was, much because of his zeal, well rooted in Vermont, paving the way for the arrival of the most influential personage in all the history of that religion in the Green Mountain State.

2

IN ST. URBAIN IN THE PROVINCE OF BRITTANY, a land in the northwest of France populated by highly independent people with their own language, amid farm fields filled with grazing cows, stands the stone manor house of the family de Goesbriand. The lord of the manor, the Marquis Pierre de Goesbriand, fled to England during the French Revolution. But after several year, when the heads stopped rolling, he returned to his stately stone home. On the fourth day of August, 1816, there was born to the Marquis and his wife, Emile, a son Louis who was destined to cast a long shadow in the faraway land with the French name of Vermont.

"I was born in the western part of France which is called Little Brittany," Louis de Goesbriand once wrote. "My parents and all my relatives were very good Christians . . . They obeyed their prelates, knew and ob-

de Goesbriand family home in Brittany, France.

served the commandments of God, accepted and recited at their prayers the Apostles' Creed as the synopsis of revealed truth, and worshipped their Creator by daily morning and evening prayers on weekdays, and by attending Mass on Sundays and holy days. My parents always spoke of the Bible with the greatest respect." de Goesbriand continued:

When I had finished my classical studies, I lived at home for some time, undecided as to the career I should embrace. I thought seriously for a time of entering on a military career, for I much admired the virtues which characterize the good soldier, and there had been many military men in my family. For many months after coming from college, I remained in this state of indecisiveness until one day all my aversion to the ecclesiastical state was changed into a determination to embrace it. My preparation for the priesthood lasted five years; part of my time I spent in the seminary of my native diocese and the rest in the celebrated house of St. Sulpice in Paris. During my stay in that house, I became acquainted with some students from Boston, among them J. B. Fitzpatrick who, four years after leaving St. Sulpice, became third bishop of Boston. But the real occasion for my leaving France for the missions of America was the presence of Right Rev. J. B. Purcell at the Seminary. He was returning from Rome on his way to Cincinnati, and I went to see him and volunteered to become one of his missionaries. I embarked (on the packet boat *Iowa*) at Havre on July 17, 1840, and reached New York forty-five days later. This was a long voyage, but I rather enjoyed it for I was always, and am still, fond of the sea.

Though the young priest could not have known it at the time, he was embarking upon a life that would mainly be spent by the side of an inland sea.

de Goesbriand, on arriving in America, was assigned to Cincinnati, where he served from 1840 to 1847. When his friend and fellow Breton Amadeus Rappe was made bishop of the new Diocese of Cleveland in 1847, he asked that de Goesbriand be sent to him. de Goesbriand served as vicar general there until 1853, when the First Plenary Council of Baltimore decided that the state of Vermont was ready for a bishop of its own. Consecrated Bishop of Burlington on October 30, 1853, at old St. Patrick's Cathedral in New York City, de Goesbriand came by rail to Burlington a week later to inspect his new domain. He soon wrote, "The greater part of my diocesans are Irish.

Some have acquired small plots of land, but most are laborers in the slate or marble quarries which are so common here, or domestic help for the Yankees. A fair portion, at least a third of our Catholics, are French-speaking Canadians. They are faithful people, simple, and good, but have greater need for priests as they have not been persecuted for their faith as have the Irish.

"The land is quite mountainous, very cold, but very healthy and most picturesque," he continued. ". . . The population of Vermont is a little over 300,000. Of this population, which increases constantly, I think there are more than 15,000 Catholics. The rest, the Yankees so called, are descendants of the English, and profess various creeds, or profess none at all, but are remarkable for their sincerity, their intelligence, and their economy. Vermont towns are small but tastefully built; all have their little school . . . or university, and as the soil is not very fertile, they have utilized their rivers and waterfalls for the construction of different types of factories. I have heard as a fact that Vermont Yankees are well disposed to the Catholic religion. The truth is that several remarkable conversions have taken place here among persons of distinguished class and character . . . The fact is that Protestantism is failing bit by bit."

Short and stocky with powerful hands, Bishop de Goesbriand's portraits reveal a strong gaze tempered by a look of intelligence and compassion, and a slight, perhaps aristocratic, downturn of the mouth. As the years passed in Burlington, he would become a familiar figure, walking about the city streets always dressed in his priestly garb (soutane, he would have called it) in the European tradition. Indeed, believing that his church should make its presence felt, he was probably the first priest in Vermont to wear his clerical garments outside the confines of

de Goesbriand, c. 1853.

his church. He also was sometimes seen in a rowboat, at the mouth of the Winooski River, angling for fish.

But for the newly arrived bishop, such times for leisure were years in the future. Within days of reaching Burlington, he was on the road, and one of his first stops was in the town of Underhill, in the shadow of Mount Mansfield. Bishop de Goesbriand noted in his diary, "Said Mass at Union Village in the Academy, then spent three days in the Irish settlement where they are 60 families—appointed a committee to select a lot at or about the village." Upon returning several months later, he saw that work on the church had not yet begun. A local priest noted, "The Bishop, however equal to the emergency, requested some of the men to construct a temporary altar just inside the kitchen door of Martin Flannery's house. At this improvised altar in full view of the highway, the Bishop offered the Holy Sacrifice on the spot soon to be hallowed by the presence of a church. Humbly kneeling by the roadside, protected from the rays of the July sun by the friendly shade of two spreading maples, the assembled Catholics, in union with the officiating Pontiff, offered their supplication and thanksgivings to God, with as much devotion as if kneeling within the grandest cathedral ever built by man."

de Goesbriand summed up his explorations:

> In all, I found five priests in my diocese, of whom two are in Burlington. One of these latter, 75 years old, has since given me his resignation [O'Callaghan], and I fear to lose the greater share of the others. It is difficult for me to tell you how this part of the Lord's vineyard has been neglected. Imagine the poor people scattered throughout the vast diocese, without a church, in the midst of the Protestants . . . One of my poor priests, partly through eccentricity, but more through necessity, claims to have never slept two consecutive nights in the same bed. Today, thanks to the railroad, he visits his parishes or Catholic centers almost every month.

de Goesbriand's mention of the railroad is important in understanding the growth of the Catholic Church in Vermont. The coming of the trains in the early 1840s brought immigrant Irish construction workers in increasing numbers. Irish migration to America had been spurred in that decade by the devastating potato blights that had brought deadly famines to the Emerald Isle. As the railroads were built along Vermont's winding valleys, with them came Irish railroad workers, and as industry developed, particularly in the towns with waterpower, so too came Irish factory workers. And French people came from Canada seeking farm and factory work and employment on the

Pearl Street House, Burlington,
converted into an orphanage by Bishop de Goesbriand in 1854.

docks in Burlington. The Irish and French were mainly Catholic, so the new bishop's flock was growing steadily. Vermont historian T. D. Seymour Bassett has said of the early years of Catholicism in the state, "It is a story of immigration, with few conversions either way."

de Goesbriand also early on assessed the major problems he faced, putting at the top of his list a shortage of schools, social services, and priests. He immediately set about providing for children in need and for the aged. One of his first acts as bishop was to purchase an old tavern, the Pearl Street House, at the corner of Burlington's Pearl and Green Streets (now South Prospect Street). Much of the money came from de Goesbriand's personal funds. The three-story brick building with a large ell began operations on May 1, 1854, under the direction of the Sisters of Charity of Providence of Montreal. The French-speaking nuns, wearing white bandeau, and headbands and black robes, constituted the first religious order of women in Vermont. The sisters soon opened, in that building, Vermont's first Catholic orphanage and school. More than 250 boys and girls attended the first year.

Also in 1854, Rev. Thomas Riordan, a native of County Cork, Ireland, arrived as the first priest ordained for Burlington. A year later, the bishop journeyed back to France, then to Ireland, recruiting five priests for his diocese. In 1859, de Goesbriand announced that a new cathedral would be built in Burlington. The old building, St. Mary's, was by then far too small, and the bishop was determined that there be at least one grand church in Vermont. Until that time, most churches were of a small and plain nature, or services were held in buildings constructed for other purposes. A history of the Parish of St. Rose of Lima in South Hero is typical:

Rev. Thomas Riordan, first priest ordained for the diocese – 1854.

The Catholics of South Hero bought a house and lot from Gardner and Phoebe Tracy in March of 1858 for the sum of $200. This tract of land, pleasantly situated near the Lake, they presented to Bishop de Goesbriand on July 8, 1858 . . . This house was converted into a church but, unfortunately, was destroyed by fire in 1899. A Catholic family was living in a log cabin near the church and it was with this family that the different priests stayed when they came to minister to the spiritual needs of their flock in South Hero.

In 1860, a clerical conference held at the bishop's residence produced plans to construct new churches in Albany, St. Johnsbury, Windsor, Brattleboro, Wallingford, Arlington, West Rutland, Fair Haven, Orwell, Alburg, Sheldon, and Enosburg Falls, and to enlarge the church at Northfield. In the spring of 1860, the bishop began raising money with the "intention of building a cathedral to the honor of Mary Conceived without Sin as a pledge of our belief in the doctrine of the immaculate conception." Stone from an Isle La Motte quarry was selected. Architect Patrick Charles Keeley was hired, and late in the year he delivered to Burlington plans for an imposing French Gothic structure. Bishop de Goesbriand was soon taken ill and eventually traveled to Europe on a journey to restore his health. Returning in June 1861, he noted in his diary, "Found Civil War raging, had to renounce commencing a new church—cathedral—as I had intended."

The nation had begun a devastating sectional conflict, and strife was also occurring within the Catholic Church in Vermont. In Franklin County, a controversy had long been seething that was destined to reach Vermont's Supreme Court and to display for all Louis de Goesbriand's tough-mindedness. In the town of Highgate in 1854, the local priest informed the congregation that for the price of $3.00, a pew could be secured for use so long as he was pastor. Trouble came with the arrival of a new pastor who changed the policy. The new priest decreed that pews must be rented annually, for no layman could own a seat in a church building. Tempers flared, and several of the pew holders revolted, refusing to relinquish ownership of their seats. The 37 year-old bishop was sent for, and he arrived in Highgate intent on settling the matter. Speaking in the church, he supported the new priest but offered a compromise—the rebellious pew holders would be paid for giving up their seats. Most of the holdouts complied, but four did not. The bishop responded swiftly and forcefully. That day, as soon as the church had emptied, he ordered workmen with crowbars to remove the four pews from the church. The pew owners immediately summoned the county sheriff, who arrested and jailed de Goesbriand. A local Catholic man promptly paid the bishop's bail, but the matter was soon in Franklin County Court. Losing the case there, de Goesbriand was fined $10.83. He immediately appealed to the Vermont Supreme Court, where in

John Lonergan.

1861 he lost again. Not about to have his authority slighted, the bishop issued an interdict concerning the Highgate church that stated, in part, "This decision renders it impossible for me to allow said church in Highgate to be used for worship by a Catholic priest . . ." The interdict lasted four years, until the former pew holders gave in.

America's Civil War had opened on May 12, 1861, when Rebel batteries fired on federal Fort Sumter in the harbor of Charleston, South Carolina. The raising of regiments began immediately, and most energetically, in Vermont. Two priests promptly received draft notices, and the bishop was forced to pay $300 dollar commutation fees for each to keep them out of uniform. The Second Vermont Regiment assembled in Burlington, and Bishop de Goesbriand visited its camp two days after his return from Europe. Recruiting a company for the regiment was John Lonergan, a native of Carrick-on-Suir, County Tipperary, Ireland, the owner of a Winooski grocery store. Lonergan promptly brought the 65 men he had under his command to St. Mary's for Mass, and the bishop did them honor by seating them in the front rows. Vermont military authorities, however, blocked sending south the largely Irish Catholic company, and also failed to heed a request from the bishop that a Catholic chaplain be appointed to accompany the Vermont regiments. It was not until the formation of the Second Vermont Brigade in the late summer of 1862 that Lonergan would lead men to war, as captain of Company A of the Thirteenth Vermont Regiment. The feisty Irishman challenged his superiors soon after the Second Brigade arrived in the war zone, refusing to order his Catholic soldiers to attend the regiment's Protestant religious services. Relieved of command, Lonergan was quickly reinstated and led his company on the long march to Gettysburg. On the second day of the war's greatest battle, Captain Lonergan's Company A assaulted a Confederate-held house along the Emmitsburg Road, returning to Union

Rev. Jerome M. Cloarec, builder of the cathedral.

lines with 80 Rebel prisoners. The next day, the company led the famed attack of George Stannard's Vermonters that broke the flank of the Civil War's most famous assault, Pickett's Charge.

Back in Vermont, de Goesbriand, determining that the war had not depleted church finances and the local workforce as he had feared, decided to begin construction of the new cathedral. "God will provide," he responded when asked how he could complete the great task in such troubled times. Work on the monumental project was put under the supervision of Rev. Jerome Cloarec, a close friend of the bishop's who had come to America at his invitation from Brittany in 1855. Foundation work on the cathedral's chapel began on June 10 with heavy wagons bringing stone from an Isle La Motte quarry, beginning the ponderous processions along St. Paul Street that would continue for more than four years. Exactly a year later, work began on the main building's foundations. The cornerstone was laid with great ceremony on September 15. "It was the bishop who officiated and blessed the cornerstone," a schoolgirl remembered. "The priests sang the Ave Maria Stella, Psalms and Litanies. Solemn High Mass was celebrated at a temporary altar where the high altar is to stand when the Cathedral is finished."

While the building went on, so did the fighting. No one will ever know the exact number of Catholics who served the Union from Vermont. The entire state sent 34,238 men to war, of whom more than 5,200 died. The official records show that Vermont regiments, particularly those raised in the northern part of the state, included many lads with French and Irish names, indicating a considerable Catholic presence. Certainly the number of Vermont Catholics in uniform was in the many thousands. Indeed, Bishop de Goesbriand, in arguing unsuccessfully for appointment of a Catholic regimental chaplain for the First Vermont Brigade, estimated that 1,000 of its 5,000 soldiers were Catholics. Certainly, many hundreds became casualties. When the war was over, Vermont units had served proudly in virtually all the major battles in the Eastern Theater, playing key roles in the decisive conflicts at Gettysburg, the Wilderness, and Cedar Creek. The long road of war led to Bull Run and Fredericksburg, Antietam and Chancellorsville, Spotsylvania and Cold Harbor, to Petersburg, Winchester, and Fisher's Hill, and finally to Appomattox. Lee surrendered to Grant on Palm Sunday, 1865. Four days later, Abraham Lincoln was assassinated at Ford's Theatre. On Holy Saturday, a day of rain and wind in Burlington, a service for the fallen president was held at St. Mary's Cathedral.

John Lonergan lived a long life and, like many of his former fellow soldiers of Irish ancestry, participated in the Fenian insurrection that soon after the war brought trouble along the Canadian border. He died in 1902 and

Cathedral under construction — 1866.

was buried in Burlington's St. Joseph's Cemetery, near the site of Vermont's first Catholic church. The following epitaph was cut in his granite stone:

> A native of Ireland, who having made the United States his adopted country, defended it in the Civil War at the Battle of Gettysburg with distinction as Capt. Co. A. 13th Vt. Regt. and was awarded a Medal of Honor by Congress . . . He died August 6 1902 believing in future life and in the destiny of this dear land.

Soldiers returning to Burlington saw an imposing mass of stone rising on Burlington's St. Paul Street. By war's end, the new cathedral was half completed. Its chapel, housing a school, was already busy. The cathedral was consecrated on December 8, 1867, with Rt. Rev. Amadeus Rappe, bishop of Cleveland and an old friend of de Goesbriand's, on hand and remarking that were it not for the Blessed Virgin, nobody would have forgiven the bishop of Burlington for holding the event in December. Bishop Goesbriand noted in his diary that when blessing the exterior walls, "I had to use ice in place of holy water." A choir from Montreal sang a Mozart Mass as 2,000 people listened. The cathedral was consecrated to the Virgin Mary under the title of her Immaculate Conception and newspapers proclaimed Burlington to be "The City of Mary." The new cathedral, however, was not quite complete; the $100,000 de Goesbriand had raised for its construction was not quite enough to pay for a bell tower. The tower would be added later, as assured by the words carved over the front door: "God will provide."

Vermont's first bishop, now with a magnificent new official church for his Vermont see, was ever on the move, a welcome guest at the growing number of parishes and missions throughout the diocese. According to a Scottish visitor to the state who heard him speak on one of his journeys: "The bishop had no notes. His voice, with little of the French accent, was clear and musical; and as every sentence was toned with deep earnestness, he made long pauses now and then, his eloquence became most impressive, while breathless silence reigned among his audience." Bishop de Goesbriand was in White River Junction on a summer day in 1869 and noted in his journal: "Said Mass in a large hall in the Junction Hotel. There were present about 700 persons. They had come from all directions. They need a church and are willing to contribute to it." Before the year had ended, the bishop had dispatched to White River its first resident priest, Fr. Magloire Pigeon, who immediately set about organizing St. Anthony's Parish.

A series of entries in de Goesbriand's diary, preserved at the diocesan archive in Burlington, tells of his busy schedule for a portion of 1874:

May 08 — Waterbury — I saw the Congregation during a Mission preached by two Redemptorist Fathers.
May 10 — Brattleboro was visited.
May 11 — Bellows Falls.
May 12 — White River Junction.
May 14 — St. Johnsbury.
May 15 — Newport.
May 17 — Enosburg.
May 17 — Richford.
May 22 — Rev. Wm. Murphy appointed as assistant at the Cathedral.
May 29–30 — I gave orders at the provincial seminary of Troy.
May 31 — I visited St. Peter's East Rutland. In the evening gave Benediction at the Church of the Sacred Heart of Mary.
June 07 — I visited Franklin where there is now a small Church owing to the exertion of Rev. P. Savoie.

As indicated by the above entries—and all through his years as bishop—de Goesbriand was approving the building of more and more churches. Some, like Franklin's, were small, as was St. Columban's in Arlington. The bishop was there to preach the sermon on an August day in 1875 when the church was dedicated. The choir of St. Peter's in Rutland sang. It was proudly noted that the building's cornerstone had been brought from the ruins of Mucross

Abbey, in Ireland. Other larger churches were built, such as St. Joseph's, a 1,200 seat edifice in Burlington's North End. It was planned by its pastor, the formidable Father Cloarec, who had supervised the cathedral's construction. But this church was even larger than the new cathedral, the most sizable building in Vermont at the time. The churches had to be big to accommodate large congregations. In West Rutland, architect Keeley was hired and St. Bridget's was built of local marble, set on a hill overlooking the village. In Rutland, the little "Old St. Peter's" church (a small brick building that still stands, housing a truck garage) was replaced by lofty-spired and

The St. Joseph's Church's bells being raised.

Holy Angels Church, St. Albans.

Gothic St. Peter's, opened in 1873. According to the parish history:

"First, the stone for the building had to be excavated from the site of the church itself. This was done by the parishioners themselves, many of whom were employed in the marble companies in Center and West Rutland. Tradition has it that Father Boylan would announce from the pulpit each Sunday which day of the upcoming week the men were to come to work on the church. The men would bring their picks, shovels, hammers, and even teams of horses to work on their edifice to God. Father Boylan worked right along with the rest of the men.

Twin-towered St. Francis Xavier was completed in Winooski in the 1870s. Bishop de Goesbriand was present to lay the cornerstone of Holy Guardian Angels Church, in St. Albans, on September 29, 1872. First, a basement had been excavated to be used, temporarily, as a house of worship. The church history notes: "Mass was celebrated for the first time at midnight on Christmas, 1872. It was appropriate to celebrate the birth of Jesus in humble surroundings as the new congregation also worshipped in humble surroundings. The men were told that they could keep their hats on since it was a cool night and the temporary roof was not finished. It is recorded that you could see the stars and moon through the roof. The basement was used for fourteen years." By 1900, only two of the new churches, the cathedral and big St. Joseph's in Burlington, had been consecrated. They were the only two that had yet been paid for.

The Sisters of Mercy came to Burlington in 1874 to operate a school in the remodeled St. Mary's Church, diagonally across the street from the new cathedral. The Sisters of Providence also staffed a new orphanage, which the bishop opened on North Avenue in 1883. The old orphanage on St. Paul Street was quickly put to use by de Goesbriand as a school for Catholic boys, with the hope that many would become priests. By 1891, within the diocese, eight academies and 16 parochial schools were operating. Serving them were seven congregations of nuns—the Sisters of Providence, Sisters of Mercy, Daughters of the Heart of Mary, Congregation of Notre Dame, Sisters of St. Joseph, Sisters of the Presentation of Mary, and Sisters of the Holy Cross.

The history of de Goesbriand's lengthy reign as bishop of Burlington is rich in many ways. Within the

Rt. Rev. Amadeus Rappe.

*St. Joseph's Church, Isle La Motte,
one of the mission churches built by Bishop Rappe.*

diocese — indeed, in a house located three blocks from the cathedral — a Catholic woman was laboring alone on a lengthy and detailed history of the state of Vermont. Abby Maria Hemenway, in 1879, was hard at work on a third volume when she ran into severe financial difficulty. Bishop Goesbriand intervened, and on a summer day that year signed a document placing a $1,500 dollar mortgage on the cathedral itself. The money went to Miss Hemenway to help with her history. Her five-volume work remains the most important chronicle of the state ever written. A set preserved at the diocesan archive is inscribed by Hemenway: "To the Rt. Rev. Louis de Goesbriand of Burlington, My venerable and dear Bishop."

One day there came distressing news from de Goesbriand's former home in Cleveland: Old friend Bishop Rappe was in deep trouble, accused by a woman in that city of having attempted to solicit sex from her in the confessional of a church. Though professing his innocence, Rappe was removed from his position as bishop of Cleveland. de Goesbriand promptly invited Rappe to Vermont. And so it was that Bishop Rappe came to minister to the spiritual needs of Catholics in the island county of Grand Isle. As the years passed, it was proven that Rappe had been wrongly accused in Cleveland, and his name was cleared. He remained the rest of his life in northwestern Vermont, much loved by his parishioners. The church in Alburg is still known as St. Amadeus, after Amadeus Rappe.

As Bishop de Goesbriand eased into old age, he told a meeting of priests in Burlington in 1888, "And now, as each and everyone returns to his own work I urge everyone to be motivated by the utmost zeal for souls. The time is short, the time for recompense perhaps is calling some of us." But the bishop's energies continued seemingly unabated. Always concerned about education, in 1890 de Goesbriand appointed a board of examiners to assure quality in Vermont's parochial schools. A year later, he instituted a diocesan school board. Always with a keen sense of history, the bishop and Fr. Joseph Kerlidou, in 1892, seized on a growing interest in the site of the French fort on Isle La Motte, where the first Mass on land that was to become part of the state of Vermont had been said. In July, the bishop bought the site of Fort St. Anne for $66. Before the summer ended, land had been cleared and a small chapel erected. The next summer, a statue of St. Anne was installed and the chapel was dedicated by de Goesbriand with 2,000 people present, thus beginning a tradition of pilgrimage that continues more than a century later. On that day de Goesbriand, kneeling on the steps of the new chapel, began his dedication prayer:

> Oh great St. Anne who through an admirable privilege was chosen to be the mother of the Holy Virgin, Mother of Christ, on this your feast day, we raise our eyes to you in heaven. We behold you in spirit seated near the throne of your glorious daughter, full of grace, crowned with glory. We joyfully unite our hymns of praise to those of the saints and angels in heaven, and with them all, we return thanks to God, for the blessings he conferred on you. Behold your children prostrate before your image; in this spot which has been placed under your protection more than 200 years ago, on this spot where the holy sacrifice was offered for the first time in that part of America which now forms the Diocese of Burlington. Over 200 years ago on this spot, on which we stand, sanctified by the prayers and sufferings, and the death of many fervent Christians, and by the privation and labors of many prelates and missionaries. Bless us, O great St. Anne, this spot of ground which is dear to you . . .

One of de Goesbriand's last major acts as bishop was to order the construction of a new orphanage on Burlington's North Avenue. The bishop named Fr. John S. Michaud, a native of Burlington, to oversee the important project. The new orphanage, a massive brick-and-stone structure commanding a sweeping view of Lake Champlain at its widest point, still stands. Father Michaud did his job well, and in 1892 Bishop de Goesbriand, in poor health, moved into the new building, which housed both young people and the aged. The bishop soon regained his strength and was back in his rectory, though in the next few years he would return to the orphanage when in need of care.

In 1890, de Goesbriand, in his late seventies and with failing eyesight, had asked Rome to appoint someone to share his duties. Help came nearly three years later with the naming of a diocesan coadjutor—an assistant bishop—and in 1893, de Goesbriand was able to go into an unofficial retirement. He had constructed a formidable record of accomplishment in the

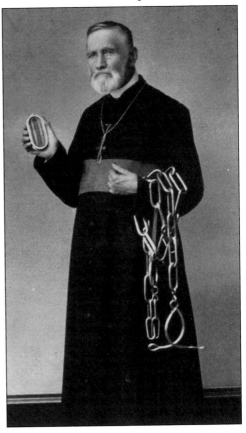

new and growing diocese, a year short of four decades old. Now there were 52 priests in Vermont, compared to the five who had awaited the bishop's arrival in 1853. The 10 churches that stood that year had multiplied to 78. The 20,000 Catholics of 1853 had increased to more than 46,000.

In 1893, de Goesbriand determined to make a long-anticipated pilgrimage to the Holy Land, with a stop en route at the Vatican. In Rome, he saw a length of Roman chain preserved in the Church of St. Cecilia of Trastevere, venerated as part of the chain that had bound the imprisoned St. Peter before his crucifixion on Vatican Hill. The Vermont bishop determined that a link of the chain should return with him to Vermont, and he took his case directly to Pope Leo VIII. A reply was withheld until the bishop returned to Rome from Jerusalem. The Holy Father told him, "The

Bishop de Goesbriand with relic of St. Peter's Chain.

decision is favorable." On an August day in 1894, four archbishops and eight bishops were among the thousands of people who participated in daylong ceremonies celebrating the solemn installation of the relic at the Cathedral of the Immaculate Conception in Burlington.

The elderly bishop moved into the orphanage on a permanent basis in 1896, stating that he wanted to be considered one among the orphans. A photograph taken about a year before his death shows him with a carefully trimmed white beard. He sometimes attended church functions, where he was always an honored guest. He wrote nearly every day, producing the last of his nearly two score books and a handwritten memoir in which he looked back to younger days, when he had first been a priest. De Goesbriand, in failing health, said his last Mass in May 1899. He died at the orphanage on November 3 of that year, cared for by his niece, a nun. A priest who was present wrote, "The sick man could no longer speak; but he could be seen to raise his eyes, as one who is praying; he attempted to raise his rosary, to raise his hand to bless those who came near; he feverishly venerated the crucifix that was presented to him. In agony November 2, he passed away the following day at 7:30 in the evening . . ."

His funeral took place at the cathedral with thousands in attendance. A fellow bishop said in eulogy, "There is no nook, no corner, no hamlet, no village, no town, no city of his diocese which has not been repeatedly blessed by his presence and his labors." At the time of de Goesbriand's death, in the pockets of a nobleman's sons were found $2.12. All the rest had been given to charity.

Rev. Mother Stanislaus (O'Malley), R.S.M.
Foundress of the Sisters of Mercy in Vermont.

CHAPTER

3

ONE DAY SOON after becoming the second bishop of Burlington, Rt. Rev. John Michaud was walking in downtown Burlington when he met a man with whom he'd attended school.

"What are you doing for a living now?" asked the man.

"I'm the bishop of Burlington," Michaud replied.

"That's a damn good job. You better keep it," said the man.

In 1890, before his health began to decline seriously, but nonetheless feeling the weight of his years, Bishop de Goesbriand had turned to Rome for help in meeting the demanding requirements of his position. The request came not long after a celebration in Burlington of the 50th anniversary of de Goesbriand's entering the priesthood. The day was a grand one, with much ceremony, and de Goesbriand was prompted to announce, "I have been a bishop for many years and have never seen such a demonstration of friendship and esteem." Yet beneath all that goodwill there seethed a growing unrest within the diocese, reflected in the writings of a French Canadian priest who was there. Fr. Jean Audet, of Winooski, stated:

Bp. John S. Michaud's consecration — 1892.

This festivity was an IRISH AFFAIR. Although there are, it is said, 35,000 Canadians in the diocese, they were completely forgotten in the festivity. A remembrance in their regard in the organization of this activity which was so good, as that of the Irish, would have been very agreeable to them. Vicar General Druon himself, probably because of his French name, who should have had a place at the table, would have remained in the last row but for the protests of several Canadian priests . . .

Rome procrastinated in sending a coadjutor to Bishop de Goesbriand. Indeed, as time passed the bishop's health improved, and he had second thoughts about the need for what would, in effect, be a co-bishop of his diocese. Meanwhile, several meetings were held concerning who should be given the new position. There was considerable disagreement among key priests, until the bishop firmly let it be known whom he favored. De Goesbriand recommended a Vermont priest, a native of Burlington, the man who had so ably carried out for him the task of building the big new orphanage on North Avenue. The bishop wanted Rev. John Stephen Michaud. Although the old man's favoring as the future bishop a priest with a French surname would seem to have been welcome news to the disgruntled French, the reaction was quite the opposite.

Michaud had been raised by his widowed Irish mother and was considered, in all but name, an Irishman. Indeed, when news of his appointment was announced, a group of French clergy gathered at Rutland and sent a telegram to the Vatican attempting to head off Michaud's appointment. It did no good. On April 7, 1893, a communication from Rome reached Burlington, officially appointing Father Michaud as coadjutor of the Burlington Diocese. From that day forth it was a foregone conclusion that he would one day become the next bishop of Burlington.

John Michaud was born November 24, 1843, son of an Irish immi-

Young Father Michaud.

grant mother and a French Canadian immigrant father, in an apartment at the northwest corner of Burlington's Main and Battery Streets. He was promptly baptized by the fiery Jeremiah O'Callaghan. Michaud's father died of typhus when the boy was four years old, so his mother raised him, eking out a living partly, as needy Irish widows often did at the time, by selling illegal whiskey. Michaud wrote years later, "I am the first fruit of the diocese in the priesthood—some older than I have become priests—but they were ordained for other dioceses or for religious orders. I am the first native ordained for the Diocese of Burlington." And he wrote that, as a boy, "the ceremonies of the Church began to make an impression on my mind & a desire to be one of the altar boys took a deep root in my soul. So one day about the year 1855 I asked my mother if she would give me permission to learn how to serve mass—Yes, dear Johnnie, for some day you may perhaps be able to assist a priest at mass . . . I remained an altar server until I was sixteen . . . I went to work when quite young, was very ambitious to help my mother to whom I always gave my earnings—the first week I gave her 36 cents—the result of a week's work for a Mr. Eddy who had a match factory on Battery Street."

Later, young Michaud worked in Burlington lumberyards. He also attended the city's Bryant and Stratton Commercial College, on a part-time basis, and in 1865 was admitted to the College de Montreal. He graduated from the College of the Holy Cross in Worcester, Mass., in 1870, having majored in theology and philosophy, and then attended the Troy Seminary in Troy, New York. Ordained in June 1873 in Troy, he immediately returned to Burlington and promptly became ill, as he noted in his diary, "with consumption." Poor health would plague Michaud the rest

Early formal portrait of Bishop Michaud.

of his life. The new priest was soon sent to the north of Vermont, to New-port, also responsible for missions at nearby Albany, Barton, and Lowell. Within the entire territory he found "no church property of any kind except two candlesticks of glass." That situation soon changed as Father Michaud purchased land on a Newport hillside and immediately set about building a wooden church, Our Lady Star of the Sea. While it was under construction, Michaud saw to it that churches also were begun in Lowell and Albany, and the energetic young priest also purchased a Protestant church at Barton and converted it to a Catholic facility. The bishop soon expanded Michaud's responsibilities to include Island Pond and the copper mines well to the south, at Ely in Orange County. In the spring of 1879, Father Michaud was abruptly transferred back to his native city to take charge of building the new orphan-age. "I was glad to return to Burlington—beautiful Burlington—," he wrote; "all my young thoughts and aspirations were conceived here."

The task of overseeing construction of St. Joseph's Providence Orphan Asylum proved a considerable one. And to the frail priest's duties, the bishop assigned him as pastor of St. Stephen's Church in Winooski. The orphanage, dedicated in 1883, rose four stories, topped by a two-story attic and cupola. One of the largest buildings in Vermont, it housed not only a home for needy children, but also a convent for the Sisters of Providence, and quarters for the aged. Indeed, Father Michaud's mother lived out her last years there. The building, constructed of brick and massive oak beams much in the style of a great French Canadian barn, still rises nearly 100 feet above Burlington's North Avenue, dominating the skyline of the northern part of the city.

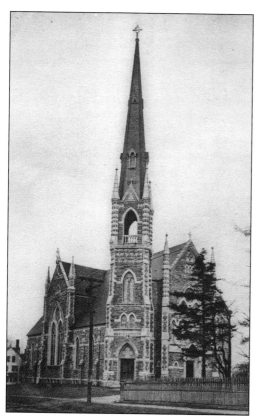

St. Francis de Sales Church, Bennington, built by Father Michaud.

Not long after completion of the orphanage, and feeling "somewhat fatigued," Father

Michaud asked for, and was granted, a leave of several months. He journeyed to his mother's native land, visiting all 23 counties of Ireland. Upon his return to Vermont, he was transferred from Winooski to the parish of St. Francis de Sales in Bennington. In 1891, Michaud was appointed by de Goesbriand to the office of diocesan examiner of the clergy — all the while continuing his duties in Bennington, where Michaud was bringing to completion a new church. On Easter Sunday of 1893, the first High Mass was sung in the grand and graceful stone St. Francis de Sales. The next day, Michaud received notice from de Goesbriand that the Vatican had named him a bishop, to one day become bishop of Burlington. He wrote, "I of course felt moved—& why not—the lowly boy to make a prince of the Church and a successor of the Apostles. Finally the papal bulls came and were dated May 4, 1892." At a ceremony in the cathedral two months later, Michaud heard voiced the hope that his appointment, and his taking over most of the diocese's administrative duties, "would add 10 years to the grand old Bishop's life."

Nearly seven years would pass before Michaud officially assumed the title of bishop of Burlington, on the death of de Goesbriand. Early on, the coadjutor found it difficult to understand his role, and for a time he returned to his parish in Bennington. But he was soon back in Burlington, assuming more and more responsibilities. His impact on the diocese was soon felt, and some of the works that would earn him the sobriquet "the builder bishop" were put in motion well before he officially led all Vermont Catholics. He soon met Michael Kelly of Burlington, a longtime employee of the family of Mary Fletcher, eager to make sizeable contribution to his church. Kelly, a Civil War veteran, had been left a sum of money in Mary's will and purchased a sizable farm at Winooski Park, east of Burlington. He approached Michaud about donating the old Dunbar Hotel and 10 acres, part of the old farm, for use as a Catholic hospital. "When this property was offered," Michaud wrote, "I did not at once accept, but waited a year. I consulted a few doctors, some of the priests of the diocese . . . and the Right Reverend Bishop, who, to my knowledge, desired for many years to see a Sisters' Hospital established in this city or its vicinity."

When the offer was accepted, the Sisters of the Religious Hospitalers of St. Joseph of Montreal, the order into which Fanny Allen had long ago entered, agreed to staff the new hospital. Fanny Allen Hospital opened in the late fall of 1894 with 17 doctors, and in its first year cared for 170 patients, Catholics and non-Catholics alike. Soon, a second Catholic hospital was operating in Vermont, at St. Johnsbury. Opened in an old house in the summer of 1894 and staffed by the Sisters of Charity of Providence, the building

Fanny Allen Hospital.

quickly became overwhelmed by local medical needs. The following year, Bishop Michaud gave his approval to construction of a hospital for St. Johnsbury, which opened in November 1895.

The previous winter Michaud had again gone to Europe for five months, a respite apparently necessitated by health problems. It is worth noting that while in Rome he was assigned a student guide, a young man from Massachusetts named Joseph John Rice.

In 1896, in a major step aimed at bringing the Catholic Church in Vermont in tune with a modernizing world, Michaud pushed to completion a procedure vital to the church's securing its many properties. That year the Vermont Legislature, at the bishop's request, passed a bill making the Diocese of Burlington a legal corporation.

Upon de Goesbriand's death on November 3, 1899, the new bishop of Burlington summoned all Vermont priests to Burlington. "You are a good priesthood," he told them. "I know you well. I know your talents and your zeal and I know that you have the glory of the Church of Burlington in your hearts. I place myself in your hands, I am your head and your father, but I shall be as in the past your brother. I want of you filial obedience. I shall weigh all my requests well, but when I ask I shall want implicit obedience."

The following year, Michaud was off to Rome for his five-year "ad limina" visit to the Vatican. En route he planned a significant stop, announcing to the diocese, "You are . . . aware of the painful nature and long duration of the malady from which your bishop suffers . . . While in Europe, we shall visit the Shrine of our Lady at Lourdes . . . and there we shall ask God . . . to grant through the intercession of His Immaculate Mother, this cure so much desired." While abroad, Michaud's health improved markedly, and he returned home with new vigor.

In 1901, the rejuvenated bishop won from Rome an appointment that was greeted with much joy in the Green Mountain State. Upon Fr. Jerome Cloarec—for 34 years pastor of St. Joseph's in Burlington and the oldest and most veteran active priest in Vermont—was conferred the title of monsignor. Like Michaud, Cloarec was known as a great builder, having overseen construction of the cathedral and of his own St. Joseph's. Cloarec, in addition to his pastoral duties, had served as diocesan vicar general, diocesan consultor, and examiner of the clergy. A great conversationalist, his rectory was a popular gathering place for clergy, and it was said that much gossip was passed there, often during a game of cards or the enjoyment of cigars. Fluent in the Hebraic script, Cloarec often welcomed members of the Jewish community to his home for discussions of the Talmud. He would live until 1920, at the time Vermont's only monsignor. Another would not be appointed until 15 years after his death.

Since the passing of de Goesbriand, Bishop Michaud had been moving ahead with the completion of the cathedral. In a considerable oversight, no crypt had been built; thus, since his death, de Goesbriand's earthly remains had rested in a temporary grave on the lawn of the cathedral rectory. Michaud ordered work begun, both on a crypt and main tower for the front of the cathedral, and on two smaller towers on the sides. All work on the cathedral was completed, after several delays, by the spring of 1904, and on May 15 a ceremony was held in Burlington wit-

Msgr. Jerome M.Cloarec.

nessed by 2,000 people. The high-
light of the event was the unveiling
of a 14-foot gilded statue of the Virgin Mary placed atop the 165-foot
main tower, a gift of Bishop
Michaud. Fr. Patrick J. Barrett, rector of the cathedral, spoke:

Cathedral with finished tower
and Michaud's statue.

>Our good Bishop went in
the year 1900 to the beautiful shrine of Our Lady of
Lourdes to see if he could
not regain his impaired
health. While prostrated before that shrine of Our Immaculate Mother, he prom-
ised he would, as far as he
was able, increase her devotion by adorning the highest pinnacle of his cathedral
with a statue of Our Lady
of Lourdes—a moon at her feet and on her head a crown of
stars. On returning he placed Mary Immaculate on this beautiful cathedral, above all of us, above the city of Burlington.

The builder bishop went on building. In 1903 Michaud visited Rutland
and heard Father Boylan, of St. Peter's Parish, make a case for the need to
help the growing number of local Irish ladies, many of them aging former

Loretto Home, Rutland.

domestics, unable to afford
housing in their advanced
years. A year later the
Loretto Home was dedi-
cated, in the words of the
Rutland Herald, "not es-
sentially a Catholic home,
as people who are not
Catholics will be admitted.
It will accommodate 50
people and will be under
the supervision of the Sisters of St. Joseph."

In the early 1900's, a great wave of anticlerical sentiment was sweeping France. The French government was energetically dissolving religious orders, and those orders were looking for new bases of operations. Among them were three that would find homes in Vermont: the Daughters of the Holy Ghost, the Daughters of the Charity of the Sacred Heart of Jesus, and the Fathers of St. Edmund, who once had resided at famed Mont. St. Michel, rising in Gothic glory off the coast of Normandy. In the fall of 1902, having been forced to close the college they operated in France, the Edmundite fathers relocated their order to the Canadian border town of Swanton. Wishing to pursue their ancient mission as educators, they soon purchased from Michael Kelly 20 acres across the road from the Fanny Allen Hospital in Winooski Park. A handsome new building was raised, and the bishop was in attendance at an opening reception held that November at the new St. Michael's Institute. Michaud immediately pitched in to help secure funding for a school building. In 1904, a four-story structure accommodating 50 boarding students, and as many day students, was dedicated, and Michaud hailed the event in a pastoral letter:

> We desire to announce officially from ourselves, that the fathers of the Sacred Hearts of Swanton, have opened their new institute, St. Michael's College, at Winooski Park. We expect that our priests will take a lively interest in this excellent work, which proposes as its aim, to attain a place of high distinction in the domain of Catholic education. We cannot appreciate too highly the benefit of such an institution, in forming and moulding the character of our boys

St. Michael's College.

and young men. The College enters upon its career with a bright and useful future before it.

The Catholic population of Vermont continued to increase, not entirely through the growth of families already within Vermont. In the years just following the century's turn, some Catholic children arrived via what history has come to know as the "orphan trains." Parentless children were shipped via railroad from New York City to, hopefully, good homes in many rural states, including Vermont. On a dark November day in November 1905, such a train chugged into Fairfield; among the 24 children on board was little Edward Kearney, come to live with a local family named Fitzgerald. Years later, Edward recalled:

> Each child's name was printed on a strip of cloth, in indelible ink and then stitched onto its clothing. My name was among them. The prospective parents were on hand with identification papers to take the children with them. I was met by a kindly faced lady who offered me a cookie. This however, was not just the proper procedure in this public gathering for a loud clamour arose from all sides and meant that cookies had to be passed around to the whole group. Because of train sickness the children were given very little to eat by the nurse in charge and so (we) were very hungry. We left New York City the day before. As I look back into this first venture into the world of strangeness I cannot refrain from comparing this shipment of children to Vermont like shipment of livestock. Dairy cattle have tags in their ears for identification and are dispersed to various places. My new parents adopted a girl of one and one-half years of age who was to be my sister. She was in this same shipment so this made it less lonesome for the both of us. We were bundled into a buggy and rode five miles to Fairfield Center where I was to live. A pile of blocks were on the floor and soon my sister and I were busy with them. She being a little delicate and rather sickly after such a trip from New York at that age, she was soon put to bed and I was left alone to explore my new home.
>
> The back kitchen of this large farm house was a source of revelation to me. Besides a churn, a cream separator, and a lot of small hand tools scattered about, there were long

traces of yellow corn hanging against the white-washed walls and a number of pumpkins and squash on the floor. Somehow, it was a long time before I believed that a squash was not just a green pumpkin.

Edward Kearney was fortunate, for the Fitzgeralds proved to be a loving family. Kearney lived out his life in Vermont. His daughter, Mary McClintock, would one day serve as secretary to two bishops of Burlington.

As Vermont's Catholic population increased, there was considerable disagreement about the exact numbers, and in 1907 Bishop Michaud authorized a census. Completed late that year, the number was set at 75,593. Anyone counting Catholic heads in Vermont certainly would have noticed a growing ethnic diversity among the faithful, and Michaud made a considerable effort to see that the spiritual needs of those newly arriving from distant lands were met, with varying degrees of success. Many Polish people were settling in the West Rutland area, most to work in the local quarries. In 1902, Michaud received a letter from Fr. Thomas Carty of that town, stating, "I think that the interest of the Poles in the parish would be better served if they had a priest of their own nationality. There are about 400 of them here . . . and several at Center Rutland and Proctor." According to the parish history of St. Stanislaus Kostka, in West Rutland:

In the spring of 1903, Bishop Michaud asked a priest of the Springfield, Massachusetts Diocese, a Msgr. Smith, who was scheduled to go to Rome, to find some Polish priests that would agree to come to Vermont. The priest made

Msgr. Valentine Michulka.

inquiries in Rome and was put in touch with Valentine Michulka and Francis Kolodziej. It happened that the three of them met in St. Peter's square while awaiting the announcement of the new Pope who was Pius X, later canonized a saint . . . They arrived in Vermont on November 4, 1904. Bishop Michaud decided that the pastor of St. Stanislaus Kostka would be determined by a drawing of lots. Father Michulka drew the paper for West Rutland.

Fr. Francis Kolozdiej went to Springfield, where a significant Polish population was also developing. The two young priests were warmly received in Vermont. Soon another Polish pastor was assigned to Bellows Falls. To Burlington came Fr. Elias Hendy, a native of Syria, to administer to the small population of Syrians in the state. Operating out of the Queen City, he visited parishes throughout the state. And then there were the Italians, whose numbers were growing rapidly—particularly in Barre, where the coming of a railroad spur had caused a boom in the granite industry. Many apparently possessed a good deal of political experience, and the philosophies of some proved both considerably socialist, and anti-Catholic. "What can be done for the Italians of Barre," Michaud inquired of a priest in Barre, "for you and I are obliged before God to do our utmost for them?" A reply came back, "I am forced to admit I fear little, if anything can be done for most of them . . . [for they] are ill-disposed haters of religion and church.

To Barre, Michaud sent a Father Lacouture, who made little headway and in two years packed his bag. Even a priest named Luigi Comi, sent there two years later, made little progress. Other tries failed until the bishop stated in 1906, "The Italian priest—went to Barre—tried to do so something with them—could not do anything with those fellows and left. I think this is the fifth one they have chased away . . ." Eventually, Italian Catholics in and around Barre assimilated into existing parishes.

The second largest grouping of Italians was located in Rutland, and in 1907 the bishop sent to them Fr. Francesco Crociata. The appointment was a disaster. Crociata raised the ire of his fellow priests by attempting to collect funds for the building of a new church from members of the long-established St. Peter's Parish. He persisted. Tempers flared. The matter was finally settled when Father Crociata was implicated in a murder plot and confined in Windsor Prison for nearly three years. Upon release, he denied when interviewed by a priest that he was about to be married.

Other efforts were more successful. During the second bishop of Burlington's tenure, the number of Catholic churches grew from 72 to 94.

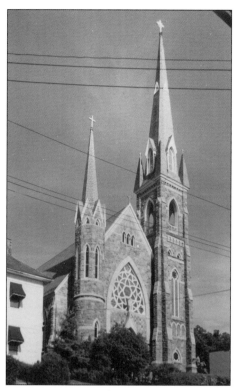

Sacre Coeur de Marie Church, Rutland.

Stately two-towered St. Anthony's rose in White River Junction, square-towered All Saints went up in Richford, Gothic St. Raphael's arose in Poultney, and heavy stone Our Lady of the Snows was consecrated in Woodstock, as was the lovely sharp-steepled St. Thomas in Underhill. One of the early churches erected during Michaud's episcopate was Sacred Heart of Mary, in Rutland, built by local people of French ancestry. Michaud was present for the opening, as the *Rutland Herald* reported:

The beautiful Gothic Church of 'Sacre Coeur de Marie' was dedicated yesterday with impressive ceremonies . . . Long before 9 a.m.

the crowds began to gather on Lincoln Avenue. The St. John Baptist Societies of Rutland and West Rutland marched to the church with the American and French flags flying . . . When the chimes were still ringing word was given to clear the church, which was done. At 9:15 a.m., when the front doors were thrown open, Bishop Michaud of Burlington, attended by the clergy, descended the steps. The church choir intoned the "Asperges Me" sprinkle me, during the function of the sprinkling of the outside walls with holy water and the "Miserere" Psalm 50 was chanted in the open air.

Rev. A. Clermont.

Church complex in Newport.

One church building project particularly close to bishop's heart stemmed from a proposal by Fr. Antoine Clermont to construct a grand new St. Mary Star of the Sea on a high hilltop in Newport. This was Michaud's old parish, where he had erected the town's first Catholic church, and the bishop expressed enthusiasm for the plans. That eagerness would soon be replaced with alarm, and at length with much anguish. Before what history records as "the Newport affair" was put to rest, it would take a great, and perhaps ultimate, toll on the building bishop.

Father Clermont proposed a 148-by-68-foot stone building that, he said, would cost $15,000. Michaud well knew the financial capabilities of the Newport faithful, and the sum aroused his concerns. As a matter of course, he wrote to Clermont asking him to show proof that "there are means to justify the building." Meanwhile, unbeknownst to the bishop, the eager north country cleric was already digging a cellar hole for his new church. Again, proof that money was available was asked of Clermont. Soon word reached Burlington that 300 loads of stone had been delivered to the site. A builder was sent by Michaud to Newport to assess the church plans. He returned with a $70,000 construction estimate. Shocked, the bishop ordered Clermont to stop construction. Almost immediately, an invitation to a ceremony for the laying of the church's cornerstone arrived by mail from Newport. Michaud was furious, and his anger (and no doubt his always-troublesome blood pressure) was intensified when he discovered that the Newport church was being built on private property, Father Clermont's own land. To make matters worse, the *Burlington Free Press* carried a glowing story about how all of Newport had turned out for the cornerstone laying. The Newport affair lasted for years, with the diocese attempting to control the rebellious Clermont, and the Newport priest equally determined to build his ambitious church. The bishop and Father Clermont hired lawyers. Clermont, asking that the diocese fund his church, took his case to Washington and the Vatican's apostolic delegate. The bishop was even more distressed when he learned that Clermont was also constructing a large stone rectory. Michaud threatened him with suspension.

On a morning in 1907, a strange occurrence took Bishop Michaud's mind off his Newport troubles. About 11 a.m. one winter day, he was standing on the corner of College and Church Streets in downtown Burlington, talking with a former governor of Vermont, Urban A. Woodbury. Their conversation was suddenly and alarmingly interrupted, as Michaud reported in a letter he sent to the U. S. Weather Bureau. "Without the slightest indication or warning," Michaud wrote, "we were startled by what sounded like a most terrific explosion very near by . . . I observed a torpedo-shaped body some 300 feet away, stationary in appearance and in the air about 50 feet above the tops of the buildings." Michaud described the thing as being about six feet long by eight inches in diameter, with tongues of fire issuing from its surface. The story found its way into the Burlington newspapers. It was never explained.

Bishop Michaud on the lawn of Fanny Allen Hospital.

Bishop Michaud, suffering an annual bout of what he called the "grippe," took himself on a yearly recovery vacation, usually to warmer climes, often to Florida and once to Cuba. Generally he came back renewed. But in February 1907, the bishop was again ill, this time seriously. He recovered slowly, only to suffer a heart attack the following October. Again he regained strength, but twelve months later he was admitted to a Montreal hospital, where two operations were performed. Fr. Joseph Gillis stated, "Considerable of his lordship's illness is due to anxiety, caused by this Newport matter." The bishop withstood the surgery surprisingly well, and his health improved. But on Christmas Day, in the cathedral just after completing Mass, Michaud collapsed and was rushed to Fanny Allen Hospital. He remained there nearly a month, and showed considerable improvement, but it was becoming plain to all that the bishop was a dying man.

Michaud urgently needed help, just as de Goesbriand had years earlier, in fulfilling his duties as bishop. Accordingly, he asked the Vatican to appoint an auxiliary bishop, rather than a coadjutor as he had once been, because in his words the former option "would be quicker, easier, and cause less commotion." But Rome refused the request, saying the proper course was the electing of a coadjutor. Receipt of the news sent Michaud back into the care of the nuns at Fanny Allen. There was to be little peace in Bishop Michaud's final months. When word got out that a successor was to be chosen, a boomlet began in St. Albans on behalf of Rev. Daniel O'Sullivan, a local priest well known statewide. A spellbinding speaker, O'Sullivan had run for the Vermont House of Representatives and gotten himself elected, all with the bishop's permission, a decision Michaud apparently came to rue. Meanwhile, when French Catholics learned of O'Sullivan's candidacy, they promptly insisted that the next bishop be one of their own. O'Sullivan the politician seized on the situation and sent a letter to Michaud emphasizing that, because he spoke French, his selection could be a move toward peace. Michaud, who by then had moved into Fanny Allen on a permanent basis, had no use for the St. Albans priest's maneuvering and promptly drafted an essay on "Language of the Diocese." It read in part, "English is now the language of the country and the diocese; when then, should it not be the language of the Bishop? In a very few years, there shall be little or no French spoken in Vermont, unless in . . . Winooski, St. Albans, St. Johnsbury, because they have the French schools."

The campaigning went on, and at last a meeting of bishops of the province was held in Boston to discuss the naming of a successor to Michaud in Vermont. The bishop of Burlington roused himself for the journey, with the express purpose of stopping O'Sullivan's candidacy. At the Boston meeting

Michaud not only quashed the St. Albans priest's chances, but also put forth a favorite candidate of his own. Michaud's choice was 47 year-old Enosburg Falls native Rev. James Shannon, pastor of Middlebury's Church of the Assumption, a man prominent in diocesan affairs. The bishops supported Michaud and put Shannon at the top of the list of three choices that they were required to send to Rome.

In the fall of 1908, with his eyesight vanishing and becoming progressively weaker, Michaud was diagnosed as having Bright's disease. The bishop promptly decided to again visit the shrine at Lourdes. There was grave doubt among his

Rev. D. J. O'Sullivan.

friends that he could survive a major sea voyage, but on October 27 Michard sailed from New York. He weathered the North Atlantic crossing surprisingly well and made his way to the South of France. A French bishop later described his time at Lourdes:

> Before dying if such was the will of God that he should not be cured, he wanted to have had the consolation of coming once more near the miraculous grotto, where ten years ago his lost health was restored to him again, and here to pray the Immaculate Virgin in her privileged sanctuaries. Now, he was coming here to ask of her two favors: that of a saintly death and that of dying on his own native land . . . The two visits Bishop Michaud could make at the grotto had helped him so much that for some time all ailment had left him and he felt he was getting cured. Placed on a stretcher in the grotto, while his eyes already glossy by the approach of death were fixed with love on the statue of the Virgin Immaculate, we could see his face quite pale and as if it were wrapped in a soft light . . .

Before the homeward crossing, the bishop sent written instructions to Burlington for his funeral. He boarded the steamship *Amerika* in mid-December, but on arriving December 21 Michaud was so weak that he was taken by stretcher directly to St. Vincent's Hospital in Hoboken, New Jersey. He died a few hours later. Some 800 people greeted the train bearing his body on its arrival at Burlington on December 23. On December 28, the remains were brought to the cathedral, where next morning lines of mourners filed past the catafalque. A eulogy was delivered, as Michaud had requested, by P. J. Barrett, who said:

> Nigh 17 years have rolled over this Episcopal See; years of anguish, toil and loneliness for its chief executive; years of prosperity, growth and reconstruction for itself. Then a devoted clergy, a faithful clergy, a faithful people, hoped to reap for his decades of years the rich harvest of his wisdom, to garner the ripe fruit of his deep sowing and wide experience. But divine providence has decreed it otherwise, and for some months, his pastoral staff has been slipping from his nerveless hands, till today we see him, once so active, so hopeful, shrouded in the mystic silence of death.

Vermont's second bishop was laid to rest in the cathedral's new crypt, beside his predecessor de Goesbriand. There, Monsignor Cloarec, friend to both of Vermont's first two bishops, conducted the final service. At the time of Michaud's death more than 75,000 Catholics were living in the state, served by 102 priests operating in 72 church buildings and 28 missions. Nearly 7,000 students were enrolled in 20 parochial schools. Eleven religious communities for women included 286 sisters. Though secondary and higher education were just beginning in the diocese, three academies for boys, nine for girls, and a single college were in operation. And the diocese was running an orphanage, two hospitals, and a home for the aged. Even though the matters of his succession and of the church in Newport were undecided, the "builder bishop" had clearly left his mark.

CHAPTER

4

THE BODY OF BISHOP MICHAUD was not yet in the cathedral crypt when speculation began, in earnest, concerning who would succeed him as bishop of Burlington. The newspapers were quickly in the act, with much mention of the names of Father Shannon, the late bishop's choice, and the persistent Father O'Sullivan. The maneuvering was vigorous. Thomas O'Sullivan, a Tammany Hall judge and a Knight of St. Gregory by appointment of Pope Pius X, went to Rome on behalf of his legislator-priest brother. French Canadians began agitating, either for one of their own or for the French-speaking O'Sullivan. Vermonters of French descent, who had opposed the appointment of a man named Michaud because he was of Irish background, were now supporting a man named O'Sullivan because he was pro-French. The newspaper *La Revue Franco-American,* published by the New England St. Jean-Baptiste Society, joined the fray with the following pointed pronouncement:

> Several months ago it was hoped that Bishop Michaud, desirous of assuring the future, was actively involved in choosing a coadjutor cum future successione. Tragically, death removed him before any definite decision had been made in that regard. We say "tragically"; this word is a bit much, for if our information is correct, and we have no reason to doubt it, the coadjutor that was proposed for Bishop Michaud was not of French-Canadian blood. And this in spite of the fact that three members of the diocesan council of Burlington are of Breton or French-Canadian origin . . .

Soon two priests set out from Vermont for Washington, carrying a petition to the papal nuncio, signed by Vermont French Canadian Catholics, asking that one of their number be appointed. The situation grew more interesting in April when word came from Rome that the three names sent by Michaud—a list headed by Father Shannon's—had been rejected by the Vatican. It was now a wide-open contest. Three more names were sent to Rome, on behalf of the diocese, with Father O'Sullivan's atop the list. Still not satisfied, French Canadians sent a petition to Rome asking that either Fr. Norbert Proulx of Rutland or Fr. Louis Desrochers of St. Albans be named the next bishop of Burlington. Suddenly, O'Sullivan's candidacy had lost momentum. Months dragged on with no decision from the Vatican. Then in the early winter of 1909, rumors began circulating that the new bishop would be a man from outside Vermont. The *Burlington Free Press*, obviously with a good source within the church's hierarchy, wrote in early December:

Young Father Rice with beard.

The latest report concerning the appointment of a bishop for the diocese of Burlington and the only one to gain credence in well-informed circles reached this city yesterday and was to the effect that the Rev. J. J. Rice of Northbridge, Mass., was to receive appointment . . . The strange part of the story is the name of Father Rice is unknown in this State and it is doubtful whether a priest in the diocese is acquainted with him.

The new year of 1910 came in with still no announcement from the Vatican. Then, on January 3, the *Free Press* stated, "Word comes from Rome that the appointment will probably be made public this week." The very next day, there was an official announcement from Rome that "the Rev. Joseph J. Rice, D.D., priest of Springfield (Mass.), diocese, has been appointed Bishop of Burlington, in succession to Rt. Rev. John S. Michaud." The editor of *La Revue Franco-American* accepted the news with obvious resignation. "We're sad at the choice," the paper stated, "but he comes from a French Canadian parish."

It may well have been political infighting, not only over the naming of a bishop but also about the Newport church, that doomed the chances of any Vermonter becoming the third bishop of Burlington. The new bishop would

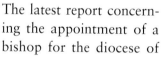

recall years later, "In 1910, when I went to Washington to take the oath of office before the late Cardinal Falconio of happy memory, His Excellency said to me, 'My poor bishop, you are going to the diocese which has caused this delegation the most trouble of any in the United States.'"

The new bishop was the same J. J. Rice who, as a student at the Vatican many years before, had acted as tour guide for Bishop Michaud. Joseph John Rice, at 38, became the youngest bishop in all the U.S. when he received his appointment to Burlington. Born in Leicester, Massachusetts, December 6, 1871, Rice grew up there with his heart set on a military career. Indeed, as a high school-aged lad he applied for admission to the U.S. Military Academy at West Point. But ill health prevented him from passing the physical examination. So Rice, in 1891, entered Holy Cross College, not the Long Gray Line, and then attended the Grand Seminary in Montreal, to prepare for the priesthood. Ordained in Springfield, Massachusetts, in 1894, Father Rice continued his studies, first attending Catholic University in Washington, then journeying to Rome for a two-year post-graduate course in theology. Back in the United States, Rice was sent to Portland, Maine, where for a time he did missionary work among the Penobscot Indians. Recalled to his home diocese in Massachusetts, the slender and bearded young priest served for three years as a professor at the Provincial Seminary of St. John in Brighton until, in 1909, he was sent as pastor to a newly created parish in Northbridge, south of Worcester.

The official appointment was two weeks in coming from the Vatican, and it was not until March 31 that Rice made his first trip to his new home. The new bishop's consecration was set for April 13, to be paid for with a

Consecration of Bp. Joseph J. Rice – 1910.

parting gift of $3,100 given Rice at a farewell dinner by his fellow Massachusetts priests. On the eve of the Burlington ceremony, set for the cathedral, Rice was suddenly stricken with an acute attack of diarrhea and a high fever. Bp. Louis Walsh of Portland, in town for the event, recalled, "Doctor called and gave bad report, but hoped to tide him over the ceremony, then fix him VIA PURGATIVE. In the evening Bps. Harkins, Feehan and Nilan arrived and after a consultation decided upon having the consecration, if at all possible, but the outlook was not pleasant with a large crowd of priests present in the city."

Indeed, 225 priests were in the cathedral the next day when a pale Joseph J. Rice officially became a bishop and was placed in charge of the Burlington Diocese. He remained seated through much of the ceremony, but apparently had returned to the rectory when visiting Bishop Feehan launched into his sermon on "The Triumph of the Church." Nor did the new bishop attend the grand banquet held that afternoon in his honor at the Hotel Van Ness.

The job of being bishop of Burlington proved difficult in the beginning for the young intellectual outsider from Massachusetts. Msgr. Charles Towne, who served as the new bishop's chancellor, remembered many years later, "The priests had decided on two others; the priests did not accept him, the people at Confirmation would 'boo' when he arrived. He had to have an unlisted telephone because people called day and night, cursed him and told him to get out . . . From 1910 the people did not accept him; not for himself, but because they had chosen two others . . . and Rome did not listen to them."

Still, Rice got off to an energetic start. He launched a series of visits to the parishes of his diocese with a mass confirmation in the cathedral of 400 people, the largest yet held in Vermont. At a ceremony of welcome held in Burlington's Strong Theater, filled to capacity with

Casual portrait of Bishop Rice.

1,500 people, the new bishop was accorded a warm reception and displayed a sense of humor, according to one report:

Fr. P. J. Barrett.

The bishop's remarks were replete with a humor which did not fail to arouse many rounds of laughter and applause . . . He said there was no greater pleasure in life than establishing cordial relations between mankind. He prided himself that, in leaving former flocks, he left many of the staunchest friends inside as well as outside the parish. In speaking of meeting the many at the formal reception to follow, he laughingly apologized for the forgetting of faces afterward and said that those so forgotten could console themselves with the thought that the remembered ones probably possessed some peculiarity such as a hair lip or the absence of a hat on a woman.

Years later, looking back on Rice's early years in Vermont, Rev. Bernard Spears, a priest for more than 50 years and an able amateur historian, would recall, "Bishop Rice was a very good bishop. He suffered a lot in carrying out the directive that he received when he was named a bishop. His predecessor seems to have lacked a firm hand in ruling the diocese. Bishop Rice was instructed to 'let those priests in Vermont know' that he was bishop."

One of the new bishop's first acts aimed at "letting them know" came in the summer of 1910 when he ordered the transfer from Burlington to Poultney of Rev. Patrick J. Barrett, a rector of the cathedral, very popular in Burlington despite some serious personal problems. An attempt by Bishop Michaud at moving Father Barrett out of the city had failed several years earlier when 1,000 people staged a protest outside the bishop's home. This time Father Barrett went, and he did not return. Rice was not present on July 29 for a grand farewell given Father Barrett. The departing priest, wearing a straw hat set at a jaunty angle, entered a high-wheeled horse-drawn carriage for a ride to the railroad station. A group of his friends unhooked the horses and drew the carriage themselves, through the streets of the city, to Central Station.

Rice also moved resolutely to deal with the long-festering "Newport affair." Father Shannon, who had once appeared destined for the office of bishop, was sent by Bishop Rice to Newport to take charge. Father Clermont was transferred to Richmond, there to be close under the bishop's eye. A priest with financial expertise was brought to Newport from Montreal. Those owed money because of the ambitious building projects were paid off, at so

Rev. J. D. Shannon.

many cents on the dollar. Thus the Newport affair, the bane of Bishop Michaud's last years, was laid to rest. Though Clermont had gone, Newport Catholics now had a grand church on a grand site, with a grand view of Lake Memphremagog. It should be noted that Clermont was highly popular with his Richmond and his Newport parishioners.

The new bishop required all priests to swear an oath of allegiance to him, as Michaud had. The former teacher exercised a bit of intellectual discipline by issuing orders requiring older, not just younger, priests to each year produce for him, in Latin, a paper on a "moral case" presented to them. The somewhat shy intellectual was indeed exerting his authority, and surely there was grumbling. But few complained when Bishop Rice named the venerable Monsignor Cloarec as diocesan vicar general and asked Fr. Joseph Gillis to retain his position as chancellor and secretary. At the same

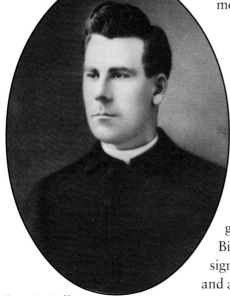

Rev. J. Gillis.

Bishop's house on South Prospect Street in Burlington.

time, the bishop moved his home out of the official bishop's residence to a house he purchased up the hill in Burlington, adjacent to the UVM campus on South Prospect Street.

If Bishop de Goesbriand was the pioneer bishop, and Bishop Michaud the building bishop, Bishop Rice might well be known as Vermont's education bishop. Many years later, after Rice's death, a newspaper summed up his education philosophy:

> . . . It was not his plan to multiply elementary schools, for he felt that his people were not able to bear the burden of providing them while paying at the same time for the education of their neighbors' children . . . Bishop Rice may have shared the conviction of some Catholic schoolmen that when financial resources are limited it may be well to apply them to secondary education; for it is in secondary schools that faith and morality sustain severest shocks today.

Soon after arriving in Vermont, Rice became concerned about a need for Catholic high schools. In 1913, he authorized Vermont religious communities to send about 10 sisters a year to the University of Vermont's summer school to pursue degrees. Educational standards were rising, and the bishop knew that to staff the new schools he envisioned, and at the same time meet increasingly rigid state education standards, he would need well-educated teachers. Rice launched his first secondary school in Burlington announcing plans for a Catholic high school to be located downtown at the corner of St. Paul and Pearl Streets. Burlington newspapers stated that the school would cost $100,000 and "will be more than a city high school, it will be a diocesan high school and a sort of social center for Catholics." The building's cornerstone was laid on October 1, 1916, with 3,000 present. Rice spoke briefly, stating that the words "To God and Country" would be placed over the doorway. "To create an abiding love," he added, "of God and of the fatherland, of liberty and equal opportunities, is our task." One year and a week later, the school was consecrated with ceremonies at the Cathedral of the Immaculate Conception, and the new building—designed in a style known as English Collegiate Gothic—was open. It was, for Rice, only a beginning. During his long term as bishop, a private academy for girls operating in Rutland would become coeducational and be known as Mount St. Joseph's Academy. He would also oversee the development of Catholic high schools in St. Albans, Brattleboro, and Montpelier. Perhaps the prime educational achievement of Rice's years as bishop came in 1925 with the opening, in Burlington, of a Catholic college for women, Trinity College. To meet the increasing demand for trained teachers to staff Catholic schools, the Sisters of Mercy in Burlington had sought the bishop's support in founding such a college. He readily agreed,

Cathedral High School.

and plans were drawn up, but the effort nearly died in infancy due to the necessity of gaining a charter for the school from the Vermont General Assembly. Bishop Rice, through his diocesan attorneys, approached Vermont lawmakers in 1921, but received a chilly response. Undaunted, the lawyers were back when the legislature convened in 1923. Again there was trouble, for the state commissioner of education was opposed to the idea. Little progress was made until the Burlington effort was coupled with an attempt, in Bennington County, to win a charter for a new college for women in the town of Bennington. Once the Bennington and Burlington efforts were linked, things began to move. A last possible obstacle was removed when Guy Bailey, president of the University of Vermont, said he would have no objection to having another college in the city, "so long as it maintains high academic standards and is a credit to the state." On April 25, 1925, the Vermont secretary of state signed the Trinity College charter and the school was born. Classes began the next fall in a wing of old Mount St. Mary's Academy.

The early progress in education within the "inland see" had been accomplished despite the fact that the world was at war. Beginning in 1914 with the assassination of an Austrian archduke in the Balkans, the conflict

Knights of Columbus building at Fort Ethan Allen.

had spread to involve the world's powerful nations. The following year, Bishop Rice let his feelings about the war be known in a pastoral letter sent to all parishes, to be read in all Catholic churches:

> The twentieth century was indeed heralded as the beginning of the golden age of peace. Purse-proud millionaires assured the world that, thanks to their efforts, war must henceforth be counted among the impossibilities, perhaps they did not take themselves so seriously as their press agents would have the reading public to believe; at any rate, we are now unfortunately face to face with the stern realities of war; we need not journey to Europe's blood-soaked battlefields to realize it. Let us now implore the God of Mercy and Goodness that the scourge of war may cease and that its dreadful but salutary lessons may teach mankind.

The United States officially became involved on April 4, 1917, as Pres. Woodrow Wilson signed a declaration of war against Germany. Sensibilities had changed since the Civil War, and this time the diocese was asked to provide Catholic clergy as chaplains. The bishop called for volunteers, and three priests were chosen. The Knights of Columbus raised funds to pay the salaries of Chaplains Arthur LeVeer, Thomas McMahon, and George L'Ecuyer. Soon troops were drilling at Fort Ethan Allen in Colchester, and the Knights of Columbus made sure that the Catholic basic trainees did not forget their religion. A committee was formed and $10,000 was raised to erect a 40-by-80-foot wooden structure, a place for socializing as well as for religious services, to stand among the barracks. On Independence Day, 1917, Bishop Rice and the mayor of Boston, John (Honey Fitz) Fitzgerald, dedicated the building. Songs included the mayor's favorite, "Sweet Adeline." Speakers and entertainers came from throughout New England for the amusement of the soldiers, and each Sunday morning Mass was offered by the Fathers of St. Edmund from nearby St. Michael's College.

In the autumn of 1918, with the world war in its final stages, Spanish Influenza raged through the world, spreading death and panic. In Winooski, one of the Sisters of Providence wrote in the convent chronicle on October 6: "The epidemic reaches alarming proportions. The papers are filled with official reports from the various health offices that every day there are new victims, and as large gatherings present a real danger, the faithful of the Diocese of Burlington dispensed with Mass. The churches are closed. What a sorrowful Sunday! We had a low Mass here for the personnel of the convent by a priest from the college."

Msgr. Cloarec lying in state at
St. Joseph's Church, Burlington.

More than 1,000 Vermonters died of influenza in October alone. Bishop Rice responded to an appeal from state officials by opening an emergency hospital in Edmunds High School and staffing it with sisters from Fanny Allen Hospital. Hundreds received care there. The bishop also granted permission to all uncloistered sisters in Vermont to give care in the homes of the sick. One of the Sisters of Mercy recalled that the houses of the sick could be identified well before reaching the door, for the odor of the disease reached the streets. In early November, the ban on public gatherings was lifted. But by New Year's Day, 1919, nearly 4,000 Vermonters had died, including the ambitious Fr. D. J. Sullivan and the Syrian priest Fr. Elias Hendy. The war ended on November 11, with 3,333 Catholics having served of the nearly 12,000 Vermonters in uniform. The number of lives lost among Vermont Catholics has been set at 169, with 114 having died overseas.

The troubled teens of the 20th Century gave way to the Roaring Twenties. Business boomed, and a Vermonter, Calvin Coolidge, held the office of vice president, soon to become president. For the state's Catholics, however, the decade opened with sadness. In Burlington, on February 10, 1920,

Msgr. Jerome Cloarec passed away at age 87. Ordained in 1858 by Bishop de Goesbriand, Cloarec had witnessed almost the entire history of the diocese in Vermont. For nearly half a century he was pastor of Vermont's largest church, Burlington's St. Joseph's, and for much of that time he was also active in the administration of the diocese, having ably served all three bishops. Father Cloarec was one of those elderly people who never seemed to age, and he was able to read without eyeglasses and hear without any aid until the end of his life. During the Spanish Influenza epidemic, he had moved tirelessly throughout the city ministering to the dying. Less than a week before his death, Cloarec had gone out on a winter night to comfort a dying nun. He caught cold on the walk through the chill city streets and died two days later. Big St. Joseph's was filled to overflowing for the funeral of the "Grand Old Man" of the diocese, as the *Burlington Free Press* reported: "Long before the service they began to arrive and when the service started every seat was taken and long rows of people stood in the aisles almost to the sanctuary and at the back there was hardly standing room. Then others sat in the balconies. The church was draped in mourning colors, black and purple . . ." Father Cloarec's body was placed in a vault beneath the great church's altar.

Despite the sad loss, the bishop of Burlington resurrected an ambitious project that had been suspended for lack of building materials when the

de Goesbriand Memorial Hospital.

world war began. Once again Bishop Rice appealed for money to build a new Catholic hospital for the Burlington area. The site chosen was the corner of South Prospect and Pearl Streets, facing the UVM Green. The old tavern, bought by Bishop de Goesbriand to house the first diocesan orphanage, and later the home of St. Joseph's College, had stood there until the college failed soon after 1900. The new hospital, Bishop Rice determined, would bear the name of Vermont's first bishop. De Goesbriand Hospital, with 122 beds, was dedicated on June 10, 1924, with a crowd of 4,000 looking on. Sister Margaret Nolin, who served for many years as a nurse at the new hospital, wrote of its early days:

> Bishop Rice . . . negotiated with the Religious Hospitalers of Fanny Allen if they should staff and run the hospital. The sisters thought it was a great pleasure and were honored to have been asked . . . Sister Mary Monahan, R.H.S.J., was chosen to work with the bishop and contractors to plan the building and services on each floor. Sister worked many hard hours with blueprints and planning.
> . . . Summer of 1924—the new hospital was ready for cleaning. A group of sisters and nurses were chosen to go each day to clean the hospital for the opening. The group worked hard but enjoyed the change. The doctors and friends would take us by car from Fanny Allen and sometimes we were fortunate and got an ice cream sundae and an extra ride.
> Our great surprise was on the feast of St. Augustine August 28th. The list of sisters named to staff the new hospital was put up in the ante-choir. We were told to

Father Gillis on the porch at St. Michael's College.

have our belongings packed and be ready. We went as usual to clean on the 1st of September and to our surprise a telephone call advised us to stay in the hospital and our belongings would be sent to us. We spent most of the night trying to get settled.

. . . On the evening of September 1st Bishop Rice came to the hospital to bless the hospital. The ceremony was solemn. Sister Bisson was cross bearer and walked in front—the sisters followed two by two. Sister LeFebvre carried the holy water font—the bishop blessed the lobby—we then went to the right and next to the left of the building on the first floor, thus proceeding to each of the four floors. The elevator had not

Mary McKeough at far left.

yet been installed so we walked to each floor. The chapel was located in the middle of the fourth floor.

On the fourth floor in the sun parlor of the sisters quarters, articles for the chapel were laid out and blessed by Bishop Rice, including the blessing of the crucifix for the altar. The bishop gave the crucifix to each sister to kiss it. Hearts were moved and some thought of the hymn "I Kiss the Cross that Weighs Me Down."

. . . September 3d— . . . The surgeons were anxious to receive patients even though the hospital was not really ready. Dr. P. E. McSweeney brought a patient to surgery for radium insertion. He wanted to be the first to use the operating rooms.

Our first real operation was September 4th, an appendectomy by Dr. B. J. Bombard. The patient was Miss Bella Brisette . . . We had only one stretcher to transfer all the patients. We had one basin set, bed pan, etc., for each floor. There were no cupboards for dishes and linen. We managed to care for the patients and everyone was happy.

In October we had 50 patients . . . Our first Thanksgiving Day we received a turkey from Dr. P. E. McSweeney and family, and Dr. Arthur Hogan and family donated ice cream. Pumpkin pie by Miss Quinn and fresh fruit by Mrs. Duchesne. Our first caesarean section was a black baby boy.

In the 1920s, Bishop Rice took action not only in the health care field, but also in the field of social service. In the latter, he was spurred on by an energetic woman, Mary McKeough, of Rutland. In the summer of 1912, the first Vermont court of the Catholic Daughters of America had been founded in Vermont, at Fair Haven. By 1925, seven courts were operating, and their members elected McKeough their state regent. Feeling that her organization ought to be playing a more important role statewide, she immediately sought a meeting with Bishop Rice to determine what he had in mind for the Catholic Daughters. When she addressed the state convention in August, she had with her a message from Rice, which read in part: "It is the hope of Bishop Rice that the Catholic Daughters of America in Vermont go on record as making an effort to extend assistance to the Catholic young women in Vermont, who, as victims of circumstance or environment, need a bit of kindness and advice in time to save them from a life of sin." Bishop Rice wanted the Catholic Daughters to begin working with women who had gotten into trouble with the law.

The delegates voted to adopt the bishop's recommendations, a "committee of social service" was set up in each of the seven courts, and McKeough held a meeting in Rutland with the superintendent of the Riverside Reformatory for Women there. The superintendent welcomed the offer of help. Thus was established a social service program that would serve the diocese until 1939, when Vermont Catholic Charities would be formally established.

Bishop Rice was concerned with the lack of churches in certain rural communities, and began a rural development program that would also flourish under succeeding bishops. Rice encouraged the building of new churches in Irasburg, Orleans, Sheldon Springs, Franklin, Swanton, Grand Isle, Cambridge, Bethel, North Troy, South Troy, and Morrisville. Churches in Hardwick and Fairfax were remodeled.

Amid the boom times of the 1920s, a bizarre incident of anti-Catholicism occurred involving the infamous Ku Klux Klan and Prohibition. (Vermont Catholic churches at the time needed a special permit to import wine from Canada for use in Mass.)

On the night of August 8, 1924 four Burlington men, William McCready, Gordon Wells, William Moyers, and Eugene White, were sharing a bottle of illegal Scotch after hours in a telephone company office in downtown Burlington. All four were either full-fledged or provisional members of the Ku Klux Klan. Moyers insisted that in the basement of the cathedral were hidden enough guns, ammunition, acid, gas, airplanes, and war materiel to blow up the New England states and all the Protestants in them. Wells apparently decided the talk was getting out of hand and asked the others to drive him home. They did, stopping en route to pick up a revolver at a sporting goods store. The three men parked near Cathedral High School and made their way to the cathedral, entering by the boiler room door. Finding no arsenal, they proceeded to scoop up vestments, a crucifix, and other church properties until interrupted by the sound of footsteps and the slamming of a door. "Get out, for God's sake," Wells pleaded.

Father Gillis, from the rectory, had seen a flash of light in the cathedral basement and summoned the police. The three intruders fled in a hail of

Testimonial banquet — May 7, 1935.

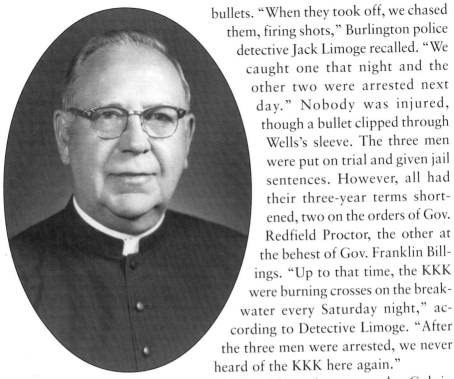

bullets. "When they took off, we chased them, firing shots," Burlington police detective Jack Limoge recalled. "We caught one that night and the other two were arrested next day." Nobody was injured, though a bullet clipped through Wells's sleeve. The three men were put on trial and given jail sentences. However, all had their three-year terms shortened, two on the orders of Gov. Redfield Proctor, the other at the behest of Gov. Franklin Billings. "Up to that time, the KKK were burning crosses on the breakwater every Saturday night," according to Detective Limoge. "After the three men were arrested, we never heard of the KKK here again."

Msgr. Patrick C. Brennan.

The Twenties roared, Calvin Coolidge was in the White House, though he chose "not to run" in 1928. The spirited election of 1928 pitted Republican Herbert Hoover against a Catholic Democrat, Alfred E. Smith. Many Catholics in Vermont rallied to the Smith candidacy, according to Vincent Naramore, a retired St. Michael's College economics professor who grew up in rural Rutland County. He recalled those times in 1998:

> My uncle was a storekeeper, and he made deliveries. He was delivering meat to a housewife one day, out in Benson, and she told him, "If Al Smith gets elected the old pope of Rome will fly right over here and roost in the White House." If you were Irish and Catholic, you were Democrat. The French tended to be much more conservative. But Winooski went heavily for Al Smith in '28. The *Burlington Free Press* scolded them for letting religion determine their vote. They retaliated with a mass cancellation of subscriptions. So the *Free Press* gave a stained-glass window to their church.

Hoover was elected. Less than a year later, in October 1929, the stock market crashed. The Great Depression hit, to be felt in Vermont mainly in the larger communities, particularly in Burlington, Winooski, Barre, and Rutland. Rural Vermont, very much self-sufficient, was less effected. The history of the Holy Rosary Parish in Richmond noted, "The Great Depression hit in 1929 as the prosperous twenties came to an end. Collections sharply declined. Many pastors organized their own system of relief for the most needy cases and in this way many were tided over the worst moments of their trouble. Father Francis Welch's building fund became a casualty of the depression. Begun in 1924 with just $150 it had risen to $4,934.75 in 1927; but the needs of the poor came first and by 1930 it stood at only $1,100 and by 1934 only $100." One of the long-term effects would be a lengthy list of unpaid bills left with the De Goesbriand and Fanny Allen Hospitals.

As the 1930s began, Bishop Rice, beset with heart problems, was seen less and less around Vermont. An assistant in the bishop's last years recalled that though he would not see Rice for weeks, he talked with him daily on the phone. The conversations would begin with an exchange of pleasantries, followed by silence as Rice waited for information on what was happening in his diocese. Rice tried to be present at confirmations in the cathedral, but time and again was forced to cancel his appearance at the last minute, leav-

Bishop Rice's funeral at the cathedral.

ing crowds of people disappointed. Increasingly in need of assistance in handling the daily affairs of the diocese, he relied on a young priest, a native of Proctor, Vermont, who had been a priest at the cathedral in the 1920s and had returned there in 1934 as cathedral rector. Businesslike, authoritative, and an able fundraiser, but also an Irishman who liked a good time, Patrick Charles Brennan was, in June 1934, appointed vicar general of the diocese. Soon, at the recommendation of Bishop Rice, he was named a monsignor. He would serve as vicar general for 34 years under four bishops.

The Bishop Rice years in Vermont were coming to a close. Always a private person, his personality remains something of a mystery. But some stories recalled in 1998 by Msgr. Edward Gelineau and others help illustrate it:

> Bishop Rice was remembered as a very strict Catholic and on more than one occasion was heard to remark, "I want *HOLY* priests." Yet he maintained always an Irish sense of humor, if with a cutting edge. Once, on a train, he met a priest who had been a classmate at seminary. The man inquired as to how it felt to be a bishop. "You'll never know," said Rice.
>
> On returning from a trip to Rome with orders to appoint some monsignors in Vermont, something the bishop was wont to do, Rice apparently thought he had found a way around the problem. He called a priest in Bennington whom he was sure didn't want a promotion and inquired, "Father Shannon, you don't want to be a monsignor, do you?" The reply, to Rice's mortification, was, "Sure, anytime."
>
> Rice did not like publicity and let it be known that none of his priests were to have their name in the paper unless for having officiated at a funeral or wedding. If a priest's name got in print for any other reason, a stern note from the bishop was sure to follow.

In late March 1938, Bishop Rice suffered a severe heart attack. He lingered a few days at his residence on Burlington's Williams Street, dying in the late afternoon of April 2. A solemn pontifical requiem Mass was celebrated at the cathedral by the bishop of Fall River, Massachusetts. The body was entombed with those of his predecessors, de Goesbriand and Michaud, in the cathedral crypt. Like Michaud, Rice died without a successor having been chosen. During his lengthy term as bishop, begun in great turmoil, Rice's diocese had grown to include 100,000 Catholics—constituting a third of Vermont's population—served by 106 parishes and missions. In full operation were a thriving new college, several new Catholic schools and churches, and De Goesbriand Hospital, probably the bishop's proudest achievement.

In 1998, Bp. Louis Gelineau shared the following observation of Bishop Rice: "When he went somewhere, for an official visit, you'd think God had arrived. He was absolutely awesome, he was so seldom seen."

5

"HE WAS A HUGE AND HAND-
SOME MAN. He looked like Babe
Ruth, big-boned and strong. He had
a quick smile and a fast handshake.
The priests liked him, very much."
So Msgr. Edward Gelineau, on a
winter day in 1998, remembered
the fourth bishop of Burlington,
Matthew Francis Brady.

Brady, a native of Water-
bury, Connecticut, arrived in
Burlington on a fall day in 1938
for his elaborate consecration ceremonies at the cathedral. Brady
had been ordained in 1916, at the
age of 23; his background included
theological studies in Belgium and at
a seminary in Rochester, New York,
and some time spent as a professor at a
Hartford, Connecticut, seminary. Vermont
Catholics had been given another southern
New England out-of-stater as their bishop.
Before long, few seemed to mind.

Bp. Matthew F. Brady.

The night before the consecration, at a dinner in Father Brady's honor
attended by 300 persons, the Rt. Rev. Msgr. John McGivney of Hartford,
Connecticut, said, "Vermont will thank God for his promotion." Brady responded, "Pray for my soul, for more things are wrought by prayer than are
dreamed of." The next day, in downtown Burlington, on a bright October 26,
15 bishops and a huge crowd of onlookers were present when Brady strode

into the cathedral to become the fourth man to enter the line of succession begun with Louis de Goesbriand. The *Burlington Free Press* reported:

> The Diocese of Burlington, of which Bishop Brady was made spiritual head, has never seen a more august rite. Making up a large part of the congregation, several hundred priests in cassock and surplice, purple-robed monsignori and black-garbed nuns saw unfold in the brilliantly-lighted sanctuary the solemn liturgy of church dignitaries in colorful vestments elevating the stalwart Connecticut cleric to the plenitude of the priesthood . . . A juncture of pomp and solemn dignity came toward the close, when the new bishop, resplendent in miter and robes, and carrying his symbolic pastoral staff, walked slowly down the center aisle and out upon the steps of the Cathedral, blessing the people.

What a contrast the ceremony must have seemed to those who remembered the consecration of Bishop Rice, so ill that he was only intermittently present. The new bishop was full of energy and good health. "He was a breath of fresh air," one veteran priest remembered. Rev. Bernard Spears of South Burlington, a church historian, recalled:

Bishop Brady's consecration:
recessional from the cathedral to the rectory.

After the funeral of Bishop Rice, things gradually began to get back to normal. Everyone was wondering who would be our next bishop. Finally word came in the summer that Father Brady of the Hartford Diocese had been chosen . . . He had been in charge of the Confraternity of Christian Doctrine and it was quite evident what his primary objective in our diocese would be. He was to bring the church to rural Vermont. He was a very good man, easy to approach, he was a good listener if one of his priests had a point to make. Under Bishop Rice, assistant priests were not allowed to own cars; Bishop Brady changed that. Priests could now own their own cars and this was much appreciated.

Fr. Omer Dufault recalled in 1998, "It was said at the installation of Bishop Brady, 'We have a father who is a bishop.' He had a fatherly way about him." The centenary history of the diocese, published in 1953, summed up Bishop Brady's ambitious beginning in Vermont:

During the first year of his episcopate Bishop Brady organized Vermont Catholic Charities to carry on and extend the charitable works hitherto supervised more or less informally by other various charitable groups. This new organization put under Diocesan control the care of the orphans, the aged and the unfortunate. About the same time Bishop Brady established a Diocesan School Office to coordinate the works of Catholic education in the State of Vermont under a Superintendent of Schools. The work of religious instruction was extended to every parish by the establishment of the Confraternity of Christian Doctrine, with its adult study-clubs, vacation schools, and carefully articulated programs of learning activities.

Bishop Brady's genius for organization was likewise extended to include a branch of the National Council of Catholic Women, the Boy Scouts of America (which Bishop Rice had not allowed within the church), the Junior Catholic Daughters of America, and the Catholic Youth Organization. In 1939, under the Bishop's direction, the Sisters of Mercy were encouraged to erect a new Trinity College on Colchester Avenue, Burlington. Bishop Brady also began the program of bringing the church closer to the people in the rural areas of Vermont. During his six years as Bishop of Burlington twelve new churches were erected in towns which never until then knew what it was to have churches of their own.

The big, good-natured Irish bishop was seen everywhere in the state. Bp. Louis Gelineau remembered Bishop Brady out on the lawn of his residence playing touch football with University of Vermont students. Bishop Gelineau's cousin, Msgr. Edward Gelineau, also recalled that Brady, after the warm greeting and ready handshake, sometimes didn't seem to have much else to say of a personal nature. And sometimes, he would nod off to sleep in the middle of meetings. Nonetheless, things got done.

Meanwhile, the world moved inexorably toward another war. On December 7, 1941, Pearl Harbor was attacked, and two days later President Roosevelt asked Congress to declare war on Japan. Vermonters by the thousands received draft notices and soon were in uniform, headed for faraway places with strange names. Father Dufault recalled the World War II era:

> People were at Mass, at novenas, praying their hearts out for the boys. Every parish had its roll of honor posted in the rear of the church. In May of 1942, I was assigned to St. Joseph's here in Burlington. A lot of the boys had gone off to war by then. I told them when they went to let me know their addresses, and I wrote to them, personal letters. At one time I think I was writing letters to 30 or 35 of the boys.

Msgr. Edward Gelineau was a priest at Christ the King in Rutland: "The church would be full for the weekly novenas on Friday evenings, people praying for the boys. Sometimes the telegrams came, and sometimes the priest would go to deliver the telegrams to the poor families."

Msgr. Francis Flanagan, a native of Pittsford, served as a chaplain in Europe during World War II. There he learned the mighty truth: "There are no atheists in foxholes." Flanagan landed on the Anzio beachhead in Italy and was for weeks under artillery fire and aerial bombardment. He served in the long campaign through Italy, then landed in southern France and went all the way into Germany with a combat outfit. "Every chaplain had a jeep and a quarter-ton trailer," he recalled in 1998. "In the field, you put a blanket across the hood of the jeep and it became the altar." Military funerals were "a quick performance," he said. "We didn't want to emphasize funerals." Flanagan saw the infamous Nazi concentration camp of Dachau the day after it was liberated. "The corpses were strewn along the fence. They had fallen and died looking out at freedom, in their striped uniforms. And there were all kinds more inside that didn't make it to the fence. We didn't expect it to be the horror that it was. It was in Bavaria, and they made all the local farmers pick up and bury the bodies."

Another army chaplain from Vermont serving in the European theater was Rev. John J. Verret, a priest of the Society of St. Edmund and a Burlington native, a big and quiet, good-natured young man who had played football at St. Michael's College. Captain Verret and Robert Davis, from a farm in Plainfield, were the only two Vermonter members of the 507th Airborne Regiment of the 82nd Airborne Division when it was formed in 1943. Davis recalled at his Plainfield home in 1998 that "Chappie"—as the men called Father Verret—created a major sensation soon after the regiment landed in Northern Ireland, on its way to England for the Normandy invasion. According to Davis, "Father Verret was de-

Fr. John Verret, S.S.E.

termined to hold a Christmas Midnight Mass. We were in this town on the coast, Port Rush, but Mass can't be celebrated because the church can't be blacked out, to guard against night bombing. But Father John somehow gets permission to use the local Orange Hall, the Protestant hall. The place was crowded, not only with soldiers, but with civilians. One local man came up to him after the Mass and said, 'Mark my words, Father, you will hear more about this, or I don't know an Orangeman.' " Soon thereafter, the matter was brought up in the Northern Ireland House of Commons, with the minister of home affairs declaring that preparations were being made to have the Protestant hall "fumigated."

The 507th went from Northern Ireland to England to be part of the 82nd Airborne's D-Day assault. Robert Davis remembered:

> On June 5, with clearing skies over the channel, the incontrovertible word arrives: The invasion is on and the regiment will load up and take off at 11:50 p.m., for a June 6 drop at 2:30 a.m. Almost immediately, Father John says Mass to the largest group of communicants of his military career—Catholics and non-Catholics alike. With final letters written home and final adjustments to equipment, there is no relief from the mounting tension. The troopers ponder their fate . . .

While the planes flew high over the enemy lines, Chappie prayed softly for himself and his men: "Our Father . . . Father of these boys no matter what race, color, creed, or rank. Thy will be done. Help us and our parents too. Forgive us our trespasses. We haven't always played square with You, but, Father, forgive us. Deliver us from evil."

"Stand up." The command rang out sharply as the plane nosed down toward a small field in Normandy.
"Hook up. Check equipment."
There was dead silence in the plane . . .
"Stand in the door."
Absolution had been given back in England.
"Go!"
Darkness and space, then the tug of the chute.

Father Verret jumped with the 507th and remained with it through more than a month of nearly incessant fighting on French soil, serving both as chaplain and as a medic. Then the regiment was returned to England. But near Christmas, 1945, it was suddenly put on alert and flown back to the Continent, to help counter the massive and sudden German offensive that resulted in the Battle of the Bulge. Davis said,

On January 8, 1945, a bitterly cold, snowy winter's day in

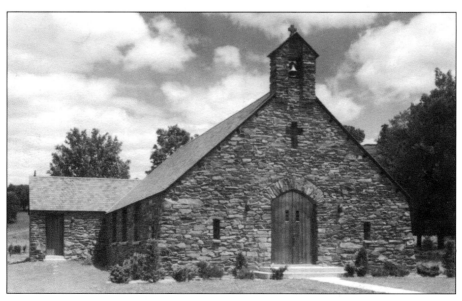

St. Anthony's Church, East Fairfield.

St. Mark's Church, Burlington.

Belgium . . . the Germans had zeroed in with a . . . rocket barrage. Chaplain Verret, having just given last rites to a major, a friend, abandoned his foxhole to retrieve a badly wounded sergeant whom others thought was dead. Father John carried the trooper through the devilish fusillade and reached a nearby ambulance, but then was killed instantly. The sergeant survived.

Vincent Naramore served as a forward observer for a 155-millimeter artillery unit fighting its way "up the boot" of Italy. He recalled in 1998 that the experience of combat made him more intensely religious, that he regularly attended Mass held by Catholic chaplains just behind the front lines:

My closest friend, a Jewish fellow named Oppenheimer, from California, came from a wealthy family. They had an elegant army coat made for him, mailed it to him. One day he had to go up to the front lines to deliver a message to an infantry unit. I went with him. There was a German eighty-eight that had gotten isolated in our advance that spotted us, must have seen that tailored coat, they thought he was a general. They began firing, had us bracketed. I was terrified, the shells were coming in closer and closer. I finally prayed, "God help us." The shelling stopped, right then. They must have thought they got us. Oppenheimer said, "Whatever you said, it must have been good." After the stalemate near Naples, we finally reached Rome. Oppenheimer and I went to the Vatican one day. I went to St. Peter's Basilica. I prayed at the altar. When we got back to headquarters, where we were staying, a shell had hit, it was a shambles. We both would have been killed. Oppenheimer was suspicious. He checked things out and found that the shell had hit at the exact minute I was saying those prayers.

The war had a profound effect on the Vermont home front, nowhere more so than in Burlington. Wartime production boomed. The city was growing, especially toward its northern boundary. In June 1941, Bishop Brady announced that a new church would be built on the city's North Avenue, and that the pastor of St. Patrick's Church in the little Franklin County town of Fairfield, Rev. William Tennien, would be the new church's pastor. In East Fairfield, on land given by a Jewish peddler who had been befriended long ago by a local priest, Father Tennien had already built a new church, St. Anthony's. Constructed of fieldstone from plans drawn by the artistic Father Tennien himself, it was designed, he said, to be "liturgically perfect." A friend of the priest, Dominic Devost, recalled, "I'd be driving the truck, and he'd be shoveling gravel. We'd work until 10 or 11 o'clock at night. The parishioners did most of the work under his supervision, sometimes 20 or 30 a night." When finished, the church had a modern look. And Tennien told Devost, "When I build the next church, I'm going to have the altar in the center . . ."

In Burlington, Father Tennien, a native of Pittsford, set about designing the new church that had been ordered by Bishop Brady. It would be named St. Mark's, Tennien said, honoring his brother Rev. Mark Tennien, a Maryknoll

Rev. William Tennien.

missionary then serving in China. Tennien instructed the Burlington architectural firm of Freeman, French & Freeman to "forget anything you know
about designing churches," adding, "never lose sight of the fact that the
most important thing in a church is the altar."

The site was a plot of woods near, and well above, Lake Champlain. In
his history of St. Mark's published in 1991, Joseph Popecki wrote, "Tennien
went out to the plot of partially cleared land and stuck a tree branch into the
ground where he envisioned the altar should be. Later he said, 'Visualizing
my parish family attending Mass there in the woods, we realized that if they
were free to move about, they would have the tendency to form a kind of
circle around the altar, some opposite the celebrant and some at each end.'"
Tennien later wrote to a friend, "What we wanted to do was to pick up the
Mass and hurl it into the very midst of the congregation. We wanted to have
the force of a bomb exploding, which is what the Mass is."

When completed, austere red brick St. Mark's, sunlight filtering through
glass bricks, and its black marble altar set squarely in the center, was an
immediate sensation. Architectural critics came from far and wide. On June
14, 1942, Bishop Brady blessed its interior and the *Burlington Daily News*
reported: "All afternoon, people entered the Church, which is built in the
form of a huge cross, to kneel before the altar in the center. As they left, pride
and happiness showed in their faces at this new symbol of progress in a
world confused by war. The pastor, Father William A. Tennien, looked happy,
too, for this building represents to him the realization of a dream."

Tennien had sought permission to face toward his parishioners while saying Mass in his new church. Bishop Brady said no, but the revolutionary proposal, history would show, was just two decades ahead of its time. Having
built his remarkable new church, Father Tennien was not content to live a
quiet life out on North Avenue. In January 1943, the priest delivered an address on radio station WCAX. "When I came to Burlington a little over a year
ago as pastor of the new St. Mark's Parish on North Avenue," he said, "I went
about making parish visits and taking the census. It came as a shock to me to
learn that a great many of my families had to live on a weekly wage of less
than $20.00, with several of them getting as little as $16.00 a week. Now, if
that is not slavery, what is it? I have been told by those in this city who should
know that the powers-that-be have opposed consistently any new industrial
plants because in coming they might bring with them a higher wage scale and
that awful scourge—from their point of view—the labor union."

His remarks were applauded by the *Burlington Daily News* and its
young and aggressive publisher William Loeb (who in later years would
own New Hampshire's *Manchester Union Leader* and make it the nation's

Bell Aircraft building, Burlington.

most conservative newspaper). An editorial that appeared in the January 23, 1943, *Daily News* stated, "When this priest speaks forth boldly against economic and social conditions existing about him, the hearers know that this is not the idle bombast of a man who derives satisfaction from hearing himself explode."

Tennien had become involved in the Vermont labor movement when a second attempt was made, in 1943, to organize workers at the American Woolen Mills in Winooski. Not only had Tennien preached in favor of labor, but he had joined workers on the picket line. In so doing, Tennien had the full support of Bishop Brady.

To Burlington, in 1943, for the purpose of building aircraft engines for the war, came the Bell Aircraft Company to occupy an old cotton mill on Lakeside Avenue. Bowing to pressure from local business leaders, the company announced that its wage scale would start at just 50 cents per hour. The company argued that its wages would be competitive with those paid by other Vermont employers. That claim was quickly refuted by a young Rutland priest, Edward Gelineau. Speaking in Rutland, Father Gelineau announced the results of a statewide study of wages he had conducted, stating, "The hourly entrance rate for Vermont, 45.1 cents, is 13.4 cents an hour less than the general average from the whole country which is 58.5

cents. Among all the states, of the North and East region of the highest wages—Vermont is the lowest." Like Tennien, Gelineau had taken his arguments on behalf of workers to the radio, basing his appeal for better wages on the writings of past popes. He recalled in 1998, "Bishop Brady was listening in. I went to a funeral in Newport. Brady was there. He asked me if I wanted to go to a summer course at Catholic University on labor. I went five weeks to their summer institute." Later, Gelineau would mediate two major Vermont wage disputes.

The Bell Aircraft situation brought the National War Labor Board from Washington to Burlington, in August 1943, for a hearing. Bishop Brady submitted testimony, which was reprinted in labor publications throughout the nation. He wrote:

> I make bold to voice an urgent appeal to the War Labor Board on behalf of the common laborers of Burlington and its vicinity in the present agitation on wage scale. I feel justified in making this appeal since three-fourths of the population is of the Catholic faith, and comprises practically all of the unskilled workers in this vicinity. The Catholic clergy is close to these laborers and their families; they know the economic burden due to low wages that oppresses them; they know the brave and pitiful struggle of these people to

Rev. John P. Mahoney.

keep their heads high; they know the home conditions and discouragement, as well as the delinquency and social vices that are the inevitable result of lack of a living wage. No other voice seems to be raised in their behalf . . .

The bishop concluded, "Let it be clearly understood that the position of the Catholic Church, and specifically, that of the Clergy of the Diocese of Burlington, no matter what rumors exist to the contrary, is unquestionably and unalterably on the side of the laboring man until such time as he does injustice to employers. The reason is an ever-readiness and sacred duty to champion the heretofore abused rights of labor and to correct the injustice done to the laboring man in the past which continues to prevail in Vermont."

Tennien also addressed the hearing, his voice breaking as he reached his conclusion:

The wage scale here is abominable . . . I have a young man in my parish who was rejected by the army. He earns $19.20 a week. He can scarcely live on this amount and he wants to get married. He can't under these conditions, and I say to you that it's a shame, it's a disgrace . . . People shouldn't be made to work that way and then take it all away from them. I know these people. They're the salt of the earth. I come from the laboring classes—I know them and I love them. They're mine.

In the end, Bell Aircraft opened for production paying considerably higher wages than planned. But Brady and his fellow priests were not satisfied. Brady convened a meeting of the Catholic Conference on Industrial Problems in Burlington in September 1944. He also

Last photo of Bishop Brady, at the thirteenth Regional Northeast Conference of C.C.D. – September 18–20, 1959.

founded a labor school at St. Michael's College. Monsignor Gelineau recalled: "I was on the faculty. We taught workers about labor law, economic politics, Catholic social principles, public speaking. We taught them to negotiate." The church's intervention in the labor movement had helped clear the way for the AFL-CIO to come to Vermont. By the end of World War II, there were 11 unions in the Burlington area alone. Before the war began, there had been but five.

The war raged on. Bishop Brady, who had served as a navy chaplain aboard troop transport ships during World War I, knew something of war. Now he carried on a correspondence with a young Burlington priest, serving in Vermont's 172nd Regiment of the famed 43rd Infantry Division, commanded by Leonard Wing of Rutland. The letters of Chaplain John P. Mahoney to the bishop of Burlington are preserved in the diocesan archive. Mahoney, a boyish-looking bespectacled lad who had been a star athlete at Cathedral High School, was the first chaplain to serve the 172nd Regiment. In 1942, he was one of hundreds of Vermonters on board the troop ship *Coolidge*, which was sunk when it struck mines in a harbor in the New Hebrides Islands. Mahoney was among the last to leave the ship, staying aboard to rescue a group of soldiers trapped below decks. During his wartime service, Father Mahoney administered last rites to 500 men. Wounded by a sniper in the Philippines, he was awarded the Purple Heart and Legion of Merit by General Wing, and was cited by Gen. Douglas MacArthur for "exceptionally meritorious service." A soldier who served with him, Joe Hunt, wrote from the Philippines to Bishop Brady:

> The men of this combat unit will forever remember Father for his devotion to God and Country. We know him as a soldier who has tramped along Mundan Trail in New Georgia—who has waded the Drinamour River at Aitape, New Guinea, and who has braved shell fire and small arms fire here in the Philippines so he could be up front with the boys. Chaplain Mahoney has often been on up beyond our front lines searching for the missing. He has been up to the front when the heat was on administering to the wounded and dying. Too full of love for his boys to consider his own danger, he has exposed himself to all the horrors of war. We thank God for keeping us in His care. We thank Him for sending us Chaplain Mahoney and for the strength with which the Chaplain has carried on so heroically along the pathways of war.

The following are excerpts from Chaplain Mahoney's letters to Bishop Brady. Military censorship prevented Mahoney from identifying the embattled Pacific isles that were their places of origin:

December 31, 1942

Dear Excellency:

. . . It is mid-summer here now and very hot. The flies and mosquitos are very persistent, I'm wearing a head net as I write this letter . . .We have built three chapels from bamboo and cocoanut leaves which the natives weave for a roof. It is necessary to travel 35 or 40 miles by 'jeep', boat, and horse to cover the regiment, but the men appreciate more than ever the Mass and the Sacraments. Midnight Mass was beautiful. The altar, placed amid the tall trees of the jungle and decorated with the bright red blossoms of the flame tree, seemed more like the crib of Bethlehem, as soldiers, guarding the outposts of freedom, like the shepherds guarding their flocks, came humbly to receive Him and the Peace which the world cannot give. A group of natives singing Christmas hymns put our own choir to shame . . .

January 19, 1943

Dear Excellency:

A complete Mass Kit arrived yesterday from the Chaplain's Aid Assoc. in New York. A card enclosed stated that it was a gift from you. Please accept the sincere thanks of the entire regiment and myself. On next Sunday I shall announce at all masses that Bishop Brady sent it to the Vermont regiment . . . It would seem that the request of our regimental motto, "Put the Vermonters Ahead," has been honored and with God's help, we will try to keep them there.

July, 1943

. . . Certain captains on certain ships must be reminded that freedom of religious worship is one thing we are fighting for out here. The ships may be theirs but the men are ours and will have the sacraments before combat . . . Landed fighting on June 29—still on the front, this report is being written kneeling in a foxhole with many distractions.

July, 1943

My mass kit is all I have—even that was in Jap territory 3 days. It is jungle warfare at its worst. Practically all casualties have been anointed . . . we are under fire.

September 5, 1943

We are still going forward in the direction of Tokyo, they seem to have taken seriously our motto "put the Vermonters ahead." We landed first at Rendova and New Georgia and are still ahead. Fr. Dwyer and myself have been with most of the boys when they gave their all—and we are thankful for God's protection . . . evacuating the wounded is becoming more difficult as we go forward. Yesterday I had to paddle a row boat two miles along Arundel Island to bring some casualties back. There are more coming now—three killed, fourteen wounded. The most difficult task of all is to write the many (172) letters of condolence while still on the front. Daily mass means everything to us here. Last night we were up seven times and they (the enemy) landed very close to us making us feel very close to eternity.

December, 1943

I was privileged to make a three day retreat with Bishop Wade while at APO 502 at the Leper Colony. First opportunity to offer a High Mass of requiem for my mother who died last Easter. All the Lepers attended and sang the Mass. As last year, Midnight Mass was impressive in the jungle. Our altar was decorated to resemble the stable at Bethlehem . . .

December, 1944

This report is being rushed on Christmas day—last opportunity. Our division held a large Midnight Mass last night but our regiment was not able to attend—due to exceptional circumstances. I turned down a leave at home and a promotion at Division to go with my boys when they need me most.

January, 1945

We were at sea for 2 weeks during the month en route to combat in the Philippines—increased attendance—after being with the regiment for four years I am now glad I stayed with them for this invasion. Came ashore with Col. Carrigan's battalion in first wave—only chaplain to come in with the assault tanks.

Undated

I asked the boys to make a little offering at Masses for the restoration of the demolished Church at Rosario as a perpetual shrine in honor of our fallen comrades who climbed their Mount Calvarys on the rugged hills surrounding that town . . . Only the altar was miraculously preserved, as we are able to live in the Church and offer Mass a few days before we were shelled out again. That night the enemy entered the Church and soaked the altar with gasoline, but Our Lady of the Rosary, still on guard, must have scared them away, before they ignited it . . . I found the Pastor and his assistant in the hills with their people and managed to obtain a tent with some clothing for themselves . . . Thousands of these poor people came out of the hills to kiss our hands after we landed on the beach. They have really suffered under the heel of the oppressor.

February, 1945

In combat during most of the month. It was impossible to gather the men for Mass on the front but they would leave their foxholes a few at a time to receive H.C. and return immediately, fortified by an "All Powerful Buddy."

March, 1945

In combat all during the month and remain thus occupied. My fifth Easter Masses were held on the high hills of Luzon near the front . . . Chaplains should not be assigned as regimental graves registration officer as I have been. He cannot have time for the paper work involved, for his primary duty is with the living on the front line, not in the rear cemeteries which may be 30 miles back, or disinterring isolated burials when the reg't moves forward . . .

On May 1, 1945, a letter came to the Diocese of Burlington that read, in part:

> This letter is in reference to Father Mahoney of your Diocese . . . John was taken sick a week ago and it is my belief that he is now en route to the States. It was a "breakdown" caused, I think, by his long and hard service overseas with combat troops which made him one of the outstanding chaplains of the war.

Father Mahoney was pale and thin on November 11, 1945, when he appeared at Veterans Day ceremonies in Burlington's City Hall Park marking the end of two world wars. He addressed 2,000 people, speaking of the service of the 172nd Infantry Regiment and of its "bonds of blood" with the soldiers who served in the previous great war. "More than 200,000 fatal casualties in this war," he said, "have written in the blood of our youth the failure to establish the peace for which our brave ones fought and died a generation ago."

Father Mahoney was never again in good health, yet he served as priest in parishes in Hinesburg and Middlebury. Failing health forced him to retire in 1967, to again become a chaplain, this time at Burlington's St. Joseph's Home for the Elderly. He died at age 57, in June 1971. Read at his funeral service was the poem with which Father Mahoney had ended all his wartime Masses, far away and sometimes under fire:

> O God of power and love, make me a soldier
> worthy of the great cause in which I fight.
> Give me strength when the going is hard.
> Give me courage when danger is near.
> Lead me through the perils of this war to the
> Peace of that better world to which we have
> Dedicated our lives. But if this service to you
> And to my country calls for the sacrifice of
> My life, I ask only that you be with me
> In that hour, confident that your peace awaits me
> In eternity.

When Japan finally surrendered in August 1945, a Mass of celebration was held in the cathedral, but Bishop Brady was not there to preside. He had been gone from Burlington nearly nine months when peace came, sent in November 1944, to Manchester, New Hampshire, to become that diocese's bishop. Brady's assignment to New Hampshire had come as less-than-welcome news to the bishop of Burlington. In an interview with the Associated Press just after his departure, Brady said, "The kind nomination of the Holy Father leaves me with confused emotions. There is deep and lasting sorrow in leaving the so splendid people of Vermont and the Green Mountains in the shadow of which they dwell. There is high hope and reconsecrated zeal in looking toward the White Mountains and a new vineyard over which they stand guard." Brady's last Vermont pastoral letter contained the words, "The sorrow of parting after six most happy years of association and labor fills my heart."

Some 1,500 people were present for a farewell reception held at Burlington's Memorial Auditorium. "Gratitude is the memory of the heart and I shall always cherish these six supremely happy years," said Brady.

And then he left, the first bishop taken away from Vermont by reason other than death. In Manchester, Brady continued his strong and outspoken support of organized labor, and there he also became a very popular bishop. In 1957 he suffered a heart attack, but soon resumed an ambitious schedule. He returned to Burlington in September 1959 for a dinner at the Hotel Vermont, held in conjunction with a congress of his beloved Confraternity of Christian Doctrine. He was ascending a hotel staircase near midnight when he was stricken with a second heart attack. Attempts at resuscitation failed and Brady died that night. He was 66. His funeral was held in New Hampshire, with many Vermonters attending. In his funeral sermon, Bp. Lawrence Shehan, of Bridgeport in Brady's native Connecticut, said, "No one who heard Bishop Brady speak so clearly and so forcefully last Friday night in Burlington could have imagined that for him death was so near . . . Those who heard the extemporaneous remarks with which Bishop Brady introduced his formal talk . . . will never forget the warmth with which he spoke of his return to Burlington; of his coming home to the scene of his first labors as bishop; of his affection for the people of that diocese; of the appreciation of the loyalty and love they had given him so generously."

6

IF CONSIDERABLE EVIDENCE EXISTS that Bishop Brady had not been pleased when transferred to Manchester, New Hampshire, it also appears that his successor, Fr. Edward J. Ryan, might have preferred to remain a parish priest in his home state of Massachusetts. Brady had grown most fond of Vermont and was only beginning his treasured program of bringing the Catholic Church to the small towns of rural Vermont. The war had hampered that effort, then before it had ended and the work could begin in earnest, he was transferred by the Vatican.

For those who recall the presidency of John F. Kennedy, the Kennedy family priest, Richard Cardinal Cushing of Boston, was a familiar and imposing figure. The cardinal was often seen at official government functions, at Kennedy family gatherings, then, sadly, conducting the funeral of the assassinated president. He was a formidable man with a powerful build, a great shock of faded hair, and a strong and gravelly voice. By all accounts, he ruled the Catholic Church in New England with an iron hand. In 1944 he was seeking a diocese for an old friend, Fr. Edward J. Ryan, who had long been the cardinal's confessor. Cushing apparently

Archbishop Cushing and Bishop Ryan in the garden on South Williams Street, Burlington.

looked to the big diocese of Manchester, New Hampshire, which was filled with French Canadian Catholics, but then realized that Ryan could not speak French. He then recalled that the bishop of Vermont spoke fluent French. Cushing asked Rome to send Brady to Manchester, and Ryan to Vermont.

Father Ryan told the *Boston Globe* on November 19, 1944, the day after the appointments were announced, "I look forward to my new duties. I confess I have thought much these war years of the day when I hoped to celebrate the return of the boys who went from our parish, those I knew and pray for. But overseas, in the service, those boys do not question an order. We preach often enough of obedience and cooperation with the Will of God. If this is God's will for me, I am humbly glad to try to do it." He added, "I am not acquainted with Vermont yet, except for a visit to the shores of Lake Champlain with my organist once. A long drive, I remember; and a most beautiful country."

Bp. Louis Gelineau remembered, "People in Vermont were very upset when Bishop Brady left. They said, 'They're sending us a 65 year-old man from Boston. It looks like they're just trying to find a place for him.'" Cardinal Cushing announced the appointment saying of his friend, "The selection of His Holiness has fallen upon a genuine man of God . . . An outstanding pastor of the archdiocese of Boston, he will be an exemplary bishop for the priests and the religious and the faithful of the diocese of Vermont. He will be a worthy successor of the highly esteemed and much loved Bishop Brady."

The new bishop was thoroughly Bostonian, having been born in suburban Lynn on March 10, 1879. He graduated from Lynn Classical High School and Boston College, where he captained the baseball team, played guard on the football team, and edited the student newspaper. Ryan prepared for the priesthood at the North American College in Rome. In 1919, he enlisted in the army, as a chaplain, and served in France with the 89th Infantry Division during fighting in the Meuse/Argonne. Father Ryan returned to serve in the Greater Boston parishes of Cambridge, North Cambridge, Malden, and Stoneham

Father Ryan in uniform, World War I.

until his appointment to the parish in West Roxbury. There he built one of Massachusetts's thriving parishes, centered on the massive 1,600 seat West Roxbury church, sometimes used by Cushing for major events when the cathedral in Boston was under repairs. The church was elegant and well furnished, and at one point Ryan came in for some criticism because of that fact. The following Sunday, he had announced from the pulpit, "Yes, there are Oriental rugs in the rectory and some big chairs, too. If it disturbs you, maybe you'll feel better to know we picked them up cheap at an auction and they'll wear for years!"

Years later, the *Vermont Catholic Tribune* stated, "It was with no little misgiving that Bishop Ryan set out for Vermont . . . He was welcomed cordially and without reservation by the priests and people of this diocese. He was nevertheless a stranger in a strange new environment, undertaking as an elderly man a task that would challenge the capacity of one thirty years his junior."

Bp. Edward F. Ryan.

Father Ryan was consecrated as bishop by Archbishop Cushing at Boston's Holy Cross Cathedral on January 3, 1945. Archbishop Spellman of New York was among the consecrators. Bishop Brady delivered the sermon. Bishop Ryan was installed as the fifth bishop of Burlington in ceremonies at the Cathedral of the Immaculate Conception on February 7, 1945, with Archbishop Cushing presiding. At a luncheon held that day, the new bishop spoke. "You of Vermont now are mine," he said, "and I—I hope—am yours. I have been a priest for quite a few years and have enjoyed every year of it. I'd like to live up to the man who said: 'I will take my work seriously, but I will not take myself too seriously.' As for my program, I shall, as far as almighty God gives me the grace, do all in my power to provide a happy, contented, loyal, and hardworking clergy and to give myself to my work."

Bishop Ryan's first official business was to confirm in office all existing diocesan officials, including Rt. Rev. Patrick Brennan as vicar general and Rev. Bernard J. Flanagan as chancellor. Flanagan recalled in 1977:

> Bishop Ryan's appointment at the time was rather unusual in that he was already 65 years old . . . Everybody was wondering what was going to happen. My recollections of him, however, are that he adapted quite well to an entirely different kind of responsibility. It wasn't any time at all before things began to happen . . . Bishop Ryan was more concerned about having me closer to him. I know he'd realized that having nothing but pastoral experience up to that time . . . he was going to—in fact he told me right at the beginning that he was going to have to rely on me for a lot of help . . . he did give me a lot of responsibility.

Msgr. Bernard J. Flanagan.

To Vermont from Massachusetts with the bishop came his longtime secretary, Marie Collins. Years later she recalled that in the spring following his arrival, just before Easter, Bishop Ryan was carrying the Sacrament in the monstrance down the center aisle of the cathedral. The floor of the center aisle was very worn and uneven. The bishop stepped on a worn spot and, Collins said, "sort of tottered," causing an arthritic spur in his back to hurt. She said that several days later, he and Chancellor Flanagan were in Boston to attend the opening game of the Red Sox season and were staying at Cardinal Cushing's residence. Bishop Ryan was heard to make "funny noises in his room so they went in to find him bent over, he'd tried to tie his shoes and couldn't get back up." The bishop was hospitalized for several months in Boston. He finally returned to Burlington the following winter, and entered De Goesbriand Hospital for a spinal fusion that took place on February 23, 1947. A long period of recovery resulted during which, according to

Collins, Bishop Ryan became addicted to painkilling drugs. He was finally weaned from them, but was incapacitated for nearly a year. Collins said that, at one point, Ryan tendered his resignation as bishop to the apostolic delegate in Washington. It was refused. Ryan kept himself in seclusion, apparently for several months, but was finally persuaded to attend a public function. Then he began resuming his duties.

All during the long recovery, Monsignors Brennan and Flanagan had kept the diocese running. At one point Ryan, likely recalling his senior year at Boston College when he had edited the student paper, ordered that a diocesan newspaper be established. In September 1946, Bishop Ryan announced the publication of an eight-page weekly paper for the Diocese of Burlington. To be distributed with the national Catholic weekly paper *Our Sunday Visitor*, the predecessor of the *Vermont Catholic Tribune* would be known as *The Vermont Edition of Our Sunday Visitor*. Rev. Frederick Wilson of Burlington was appointed editor.

But accomplishments were few in Bishop Ryan's early time in Vermont. The *Catholic Tribune* later noted:

> His first two years were discouraging indeed. The inevitable infirmities of advancing age began to overtake him during several months of enforced rest and his friends began to wonder if the burden which had been laid upon him might not prove too heavy for him to bear. Presently, as if by divine rejuvenation, his strength returned. He gained a clear and detailed picture of the needs of his diocese and of the possibilities of extending the influence of the Church which were opened up to him in his new position.

With the return of health, Ryan resumed a busy schedule, certainly busy for a man of his years. In 1946, Vermont Catholic Charities, with the blessings of Bishop Ryan, had opened a camp for Catholic boys, Camp Holy Cross, on the shores of Lake Champlain's Malletts Bay. (A dozen years later Camp Tara, for Catholic girls, began operating nearby.) On August 28, 1948, Bishop Ryan convened at Camp Holy Cross the first Catholic Rural Life Institute ever held in the eastern United States. At the time, in the postwar years, much attention nationally was being directed at trying to bring more modern living conditions, including electricity, to the nation's generally poor rural areas. Ryan opened the weeklong conference with an address to an audience that included many young men studying for the priesthood. He said, "The future of the church in Vermont, as well as in other states, lies not in the urban population, but in the rural areas. We can only do so much as

Redemptorist Monastery at Bradford.

Bishops, the actual work must be done by men like yourselves who will be in the rural parishes. We trust that through your discussions and instructions this week you will be better prepared to meet the challenges found in working for the salvation of souls in rural areas." The bishop emphasized his point by stating that the Diocese of Burlington had made a $300,000 investment in 14 mission churches and chapels throughout the state.

Seeing it as a key part of his rural program, Bishop Ryan embarked on an effort to convince more religious orders to locate in Vermont. Their members, he believed, could work to bring the church into backcountry Vermont. One area of prime concern was the Connecticut River Valley, between St. Johnsbury and White River Junction, where there was no resident priest. A history of Bradford described the coming of a religious order to that valley town:

> Not long after . . . Edward F. Ryan was named Bishop of the Catholic Church in Vermont, he found that the diocese was quite short of priests. On April 22, 1945 he wrote to Father Provincial Rev. Michael A. Gearin, asking the Redemptorist Fathers to enter the Diocese and serve the area from Barnet to Wilder along the Connecticut River and westward for about 15 miles. This request was made to the Redemptorists because they are priests and brothers . . .

whose purpose is to care for areas which are neglected for lack of priests . . . Two Redemptionists came here on June 30, 1945 to survey the situation. Fathers Joseph E. Scannell and Joseph Rocheleau took up temporary residence at the Bradford Inn . . . and immediately began to take a census of the area, some 45 miles long and containing approximately 800 square miles. As a result of their survey, they recommended that the parish church and the rectory be established in Bradford, with auxiliary chapels in Wells River, Norwich and South Strafford. Meanwhile, the priests lived at the Bradford Inn. They had Sunday Mass there in the dining room and in town halls, theaters and elsewhere . . . On Christmas eve, 1945, the midnight mass was celebrated at the inn, as it was again in December, 1946. In mid-Au-

Original Carthusian Monastery, Whitingham — 1951.

gust the parish at Bradford was accepted by the Redemptorist Community and not long after the building of the parish church and rectory at Bradford and chapel at Wells River was undertaken. Later, modern-type chapels were erected in South Strafford and Norwich.

Land on the "Upper Plain," just north of Bradford village, was purchased for the Redemptorist Fathers' main church. Gov. Mortimer Proctor and other dignitaries were present on a July day in 1946 for the laying of the cornerstone. A telegram from President Truman was read in which he took note of the "glory of a new house of God along the Connecticut River in Vermont."

Also to Vermont, at the behest of Ryan, came the Carthusian Fathers, establishing at Whitingham their first foundation in the Western Hemisphere; the Benedictines, locating in Weston; the Daughters of Charity of the Most Precious Blood, who came from war-ravaged Italy to Randolph; the Sisters of St. Joan of Arc, who located in Burlington; the Sisters of Notre Dame, who opened the Immaculate Heart of Mary School in Rutland; and the Carmelite Sisters, who founded a "Carmel" in Williston.

For help in staffing the new churches, Bishop Ryan turned to his beloved Massachusetts, where there was an excess of young priests. With the help of old friend Cardinal Cushing, many of those young fathers soon found themselves headed for the Green Mountains of Vermont. Fr. Omer Dufault recalled in 1998:

> He was bound he was going to have a church in every small town in Vermont. He opened many new parishes. I was assigned as a parish priest to Hyde Park. I was told I was expected to build a church in Johnson, the next town over. Father Flanagan visited me about a year later and said, "The bishop wonders what you are doing about that church in Johnson?" So I knew he was serious. So I built one, of poured concrete. It's still there. I started a parish up in Eden, in a school building we bought for $500. We nearly froze in there. But we were young then. No distance was too great, no hill too high.

Louis Gelineau recalled in 1998, "Bishop Ryan became a grandfather figure in Vermont, but a good one. He went into these little towns in Vermont that had no churches. He became a lover of those little towns, and they loved him. He got to know the state well and became a Vermonter. But he always loved to go back to Boston."

Vincent Naramore also remembered Ryan, "He had a nice way about him. He was really good with kids. He got around Vermont. The priests liked him; they called him, though perhaps not to his face, Big Ed."

"Big Ed," by the late 1940s, was going full speed ahead, and churches seemed to be springing up everywhere. In 1945, the new parish of Our Lady of Perpetual Help was founded in Bradford, the new church of St. Denis was erected in Pittsfield, and the following missions were established: St. John

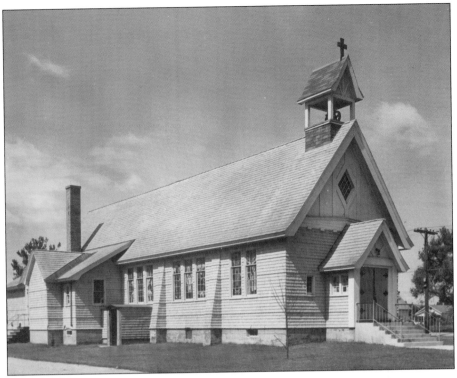

Morrisville church, one of the small rural parishes founded by Bishop Ryan.

the Apostle in Johnson, St. Francis of Assisi in Norwich, Our Lady of Fatima in South Strafford, and St. Eugene in Wells River.

New parishes were formed in 1946: St. Joseph in Chester, Holy Cross in Morrisville, St. Jude in Hinesburg, and St. Edward in Derby Line. The missions of St. Edmund in Saxton's River, Our Lady of Hope in Wardsboro, St. John Berchmans in West Dummerston, Our Lady of the Valley in Townshend, St. Francis Cabrini in West Pawlet, St. Benedict Labre in West Charleston, and St. Francis Cabrini in East Barre were begun. New churches were opened in Norwich, South Strafford, Wells River, West Pawlet, Townshend, West Dummerston, and Johnson.

In 1947, one new mission, St. Gabriel in Eden, began, while new churches opened in Bradford, Chester, Derby Line, and West Charleston. The next year, the parishes of St. Anthony in East Fairfield and St. Monica in Barre began. The new missions of St. Edward at Williamstown and St. Edmund at Fort Ethan Allen commenced, while Forestdale, Hinesburg, and East Barre opened new houses of worship. In 1949, the first Mass was said at the Church of the Blessed Sacrament in Stowe. In 1950, the following parishes were created: Holy Cross at Malletts Bay, Immaculate Heart of Mary at Williston, and St. Anthony in Bethel. A new church was blessed in Wilmington and a mission, Our Lady of Fatima, began at Craftsbury in the north.

In 1999, Msgr. Edwin Buckley looked back to a time when he was a young priest and had founded a Vermont parish, in the Windsor County town of Chester. The story really began, he said, in his native Massachusetts. "It was the depression," he recalled, "I didn't have any money." But Buckley said he heard of opportunity in Vermont and came north for a meeting with Bishop Rice:

> The bishop was familiar with Pittsfield in Massachusetts, my hometown, he'd been stationed there once. He told me that being a priest in Vermont would be a lot different than being a priest in Pittsfield. He told me to go up to that little village north of Pittsfield, walk through it, and see if I thought I could be happy there the rest of my life. I said, "You mean Williamstown?" He said, "No, that's too big." I said, "Are you talking about Lanesboro?" "Yes," he said. Lanesboro was so small you'd go through it and not even think about it. He said that if I could be happy in a place like that, he'd take me. I went back to Pittsfield and I went to Lanesboro, and it seemed okay to me.

Fr. Edwin Buckley and parishioners in front of the future church in Chester.

Buckley accepted and went to Montreal for six years of seminary. His first Vermont assignment was in Brattleboro, where he taught at St. Michael's High School.

It was wartime and we wanted to start a school band. So we raffled off a car, a new car. You couldn't get a new car during the war. Everybody bought tickets. Then I get word that I'm being sent to Chester. There isn't even a church there. I didn't have a car so I spent $10 on raffle tickets. I knew the Lord would have me win because He'd gotten me into this situation. But I didn't win. The people in the parish gave me a car the day I left and the new band played the only thing it had learned for me, the "Notre Dame Fight Song."

Father Buckley drove his new car to Chester. There he received a cold welcome. Anti-Catholic sentiment was rampant, and it was six days before anyone he met on the street would speak to him. The diocese had bought a house in Chester for its new priest, but Father Buckley had to wait for the old couple living there to move out. "I met her on the street one day," Buckley remembered, "and she said they were about to move. She asked me if I was going to live in that house all by myself and I said I was. She said that a nice young man like me ought to find a nice young lady and get married. I said, 'Yeah, that would fix everything.'"

Church in Chester.

There being no church in Chester, Father Buckley got permission from the owners of the Chester Inn to say mass in the dining room on Sunday mornings between breakfast and lunch. "We had eight people the first few weeks," he said, "and you could hear the noise of the dishes being washed." Finally, construction of a Catholic church was begun. The walls were raised and the roof put on. But it all came to a halt when a notice came from the town of Chester stating that the building was violating zoning regulations. Buckley went back to Brattleboro and sought legal help. It came from Atty. Ernest Gibson, just elected governor of Vermont, who had not yet taken office. "Ernest Gibson said," Buckley recalled in 1999, "'There's no place for this kind of thing in Vermont.'" Gibson agreed to represent the church, and a zoning variance was quickly granted. The building of the church was completed. World War II ended and a grand victory parade was planned in New York City. "I flew down with Governor Gibson, on the state plane," Father Buckley said. "The new band from my old school, St. Michael's in Brattleboro, in Governor Gibson's hometown, led the Vermont contingent up Broadway."

All the while, Father Buckley was in search of parishioners, and one day he met with a farmer in the village. Buckley had heard that the man had a Catholic background. "He told me, 'Hell yes, I'm a Catholic. But I don't remember anything about it, except there used to be a big picnic.'" What Buckley finally deduced was that the man was recalling long-ago days when an itinerant priest came to Chester to say Mass, in a field outside the town, and local Catholics brought a picnic lunch. Buckley spent more than a decade in Chester. When he left for White River Junction, the church was paid for and the parish, St. Joseph's, had begun to thrive.

In 1951, Bishop Ryan made an appeal to Vermont Catholics for added financial support for his rural program. He wrote:

> The happy promise of the harvest which Vermont's green fields holds today reminds us of the spiritual harvest of souls which those same rural areas should yield. Where the opportunities for religion are available, the Catholics of our farming communities are exemplary. Unfortunately, however, in many instances the Catholic families are too few to build and support even a modest chapel. They must live far from the church, far from the life-giving sacraments of their religion. Frequently, it is impossible for them to make such a trip because of distance and weather conditions. It is important that we act promptly to provide these people with religious facilities lest, like ripened wheat left standing in the field, they be lost to the harvest forever.

He went on to list some recent successes.

> We have provided a new chapel named Our Lady of Fatima at Wilmington, as well as a new chapel in honor of St. John Gabriel's at Eden. We have procured land and a house at Craftsbury and at Greensboro Bend. The house at Craftsbury will be made into a chapel and the house at Greensboro Bend a rectory. We have bought land at Canaan upon which a chapel will be built this summer. We have purchased land at Saxton's River for a chapel . . . Therefore, in the name of the many Vermont Catholics of rural communities who cannot carry the burden alone, we call for assistance in this great spiritual work. . .Behold the fields are ripe for the harvest' (John 4:35)."

New churches opened in Williston and Craftsbury in 1951. In 1952, the new parish of the Assumption of the Blessed Virgin began in Canaan, and a church opened in Saxton's River. The following year brought forth churches in Wardsboro, East Berkshire, and Canaan. Blessed Sacrament Parish in Stowe and St. Michael's Parish in Greensboro Bend were founded in 1954. Windsor and Richmond also opened new churches that year.

Vincent Naramore was a student at St. Michael's College during a portion of Ryan's years as bishop. He recalled that the bishop had a distinct Massachusetts accent and that, when called upon to speak, he would begin by saying, "I just want to say a few words," but would often go on at considerable length. Naramore said that a certain professor at St. Michael's could imitate the bishop and his accent perfectly. "When the bishop got up to speak there, some students would start to giggle."

There may have been giggles, but Bishop Ryan was totally serious on Friday, June 4, 1954, when he delivered the commencement address at St. Michael's College, just after having been awarded an honorary degree. Speaking from a typed text, he said:

> In the realm of civic affairs, my counsel to you is the same as that of your church, namely that you interest yourself in all matters that vitally affect the nation and its citizens. Perhaps one of the saddest and most discouraging happenings of modern times was the recent legislation of the Supreme Court of the United States and the Vermont State Board of Education abolishing the teaching of the truths of God and religion in our public schools. This was done under the

pretense of defending the first amendment of the Constitution and with the claim that it was keeping intact the wall separating church and state. If one reads the first amendment, it says, "Congress shall make no laws respecting an establishment of religion or prohibiting the free exercise thereof." What this had to do with religious education is certainly not clear to the lay mind . . . Certainly Madison who gets the credit for writing the first amendment never had it in his mind to exclude the teaching of religion in the schools, and neither did Thomas Jefferson.

Then Ryan turned to another matter, speaking from notes hastily scribbled at the bottom of his prepared text. "An up-to-the-minute example of the abdication of moral concepts," he began, "and the putting aside the rights of God over life is to be found in the statement of the dean of the Vermont Medical School, as reported in today's *Burlington Free Press*. If the learned doctor is quoted correctly, he made human beings little different from animals, saying, according to the press, it is my feeling that we might consider doing for human beings what we do for animals. We do not allow our pets to suffer when they are helpless or injured."

David Jennings in Korea.

The bishop was referring to Dr. William E. Brown, dean of the UVM Medical School, who had recently spoken in favor of legalizing euthanasia. The so-called eugenics movement had many years before taken root within some quarters of the state university. *Eugenics* is defined by *Webster's Dictionary* as "a science that deals with the improvement (as by control or human mating) of hereditary qualities of a race or breed." The chief advocate at the university had been Prof. Harry Perkins, head of the Fleming Museum, who years before had been instrumental in pushing a human sterilization law to enactment in the Vermont Legislature. The eugenics movement had never been challenged by the clergy in Vermont until that day at St. Michael's, when Bishop Ryan decided it had all gone too far.

Within the bishop's audience that spring day were certainly a goodly number of young men and women who would soon find themselves in military uniform. The Korean War had begun in 1950, and the United Nations quickly responded by sending troops to its allies in South Korea. Before the war ended, 20,000 Vermonters would serve in the Korean War. Among them was David Jennings of Burlington, who in the summer of 1949 had struck off on a boyhood adventure, hitchhiking with his friend John McSweeney (later to be a monsignor) from Burlington to Cedar Rapids, Iowa, in just 81 hours. Less than two years later, Jennings was a first lieutenant in the U.S. Army and commanding an infantry company in combat, in a mountainous area of Korea known as the Punch Bowl. Jennings faithfully wrote letters to his parents, James and Madine Jennings of Burlington, letters he always addressed "Dear Mom and Dad."

November 4, 1952

Dear Mom and Dad,

As darkness was coming on, our long file of trucks started the long climb over Punch Bowl Pass. Luckily, I don't put much faith in omens of any sort for the sky toward which we were inching had a particularly evil look about it. Large billous clouds, their lower edges trailing smoke-like fringes, boiled low over the pass, and the mustard yellow storm line, characteristic of violent storms, reminded me of another such storm I had witnessed one night in the midst of Iowa cornlands . . . At the height of the pass we came under enemy observation and the truck lights were turned off.

Tonight we had a very detailed and dangerous patrol out . . . so I decided to stay up all night to insure they got fire support from the mortars and arty if they needed it . . . It is now 5:00 a. m. The patrols came in about two hours ago and I got Sgt. Schleeter, 1st Sgt. to come up here and pull phone guard . . . They didn't run into anything in spite of the fact that it got within 60 yards of the base of "No Name" Ridge and they had orders to make contact . . . All of us experience fear several times a day . . . At any given moment you can just about take your choice of 45 mm, 76 mm, 60 & 82 & 120 mm mortar, some heavy and, as yet, unidentified artillery and, if they spot you moving they may throw in a little staccato in the form of a machine gun. All in all, it's a lively life, if a dangerous one.

December 7, 1952

Thanks a million . . . you couldn't have sent a more timely birthday present. And Mom, I received your wonderful card yesterday. You enquired about our Thanksgiving here on the line? Well, we had turkey and all the fixins and goodies to go along with it . . . During the daylight hours the past three days the mercury hovered at 0 and at night it dropped to a low of -10 . . . As usual when I get worn out, last week I came down with a cold and cough. One unique feature of this was that I coughed so hard during one spell that I broke one of my lower ribs, of all the ridiculous things to happen. I'm still taped up and itch like hell . . . Give my love to Nanno & Aunt Nell and all the folks. I now have only 19 points and even if I'm lucky it doesn't look like I'll get out of here before April, so keep the mail coming—it's going to be a long winter.

Loads of love,

Dave

Groundbreaking for St. Joseph Pavilion,
Bishop De Goesbriand Memorial Hospital:
Msgr. Brennan, Bishop Ryan with shovel,
Mother Anna Collins at right.

Then came the worst news:

December 8, 1952

A few hours ago your son was selected to pay the supreme sacrifice for his country. Now that he has fulfilled his mission on earth I am certain and positive that he will find his place with God. I have lost a great friend, you a Son. Let us comfort each other and re-member his great-

ness. I shall never forget his kindness, thoughtfulness, courage, and devotion to duty. Dave will live forever in my memory as one of the greatest . . .

Sincerely,
Sgt. Richard G. Schleeter

January 27, 1953

Dave died like a man, giving his life for other men I had taken out on a daylight patrol. We were hit by the Reds and in a matter of min-utes, I was the only member of the patrol that had not been hit. I called back to our lines to tell them what

Mother Collins, Sister Superior,
De Goesbriand Hospital.

had happened. Dave told me he would be right out with help . . . As he neared our position, I again warned him but he came on, shells landing all around him. Dave made it to where we were with three litter teams. As we laid side by side in the snow trying to figure out how we would get the wounded out, a call came in on the radio. I moved over about a foot to answer it, still not more than two feet from Dave, when a mortar shell landed between us. It killed Dave outright, he never knew what hit him. God made the choice, I did not even get a scratch . . .

Dave was a fine officer and a fine Catholic. In the six months I knew him, I never saw him miss Mass. I myself am not too good a Catholic but it was an inspiration to both myself and the men of the company to see such devotion. I can't help but feel God took Dave because he had an express ticket to heaven while I would have had to make a few stops along the way. I put Dave in for the Silver Star . . .

Roy J. Herte
1st Lt. Inf.

The Korean War, officially termed by the U.N. a "police action," did not drain national manpower and resources as did World War II. Still, Lieutenant Jennings was one of more than 50,000 Americans who gave their lives.

Msgr. John M. Kennedy, Christ the King, Rutland.

Because of the war, Bishop Ryan had been forced to curtail his ambitious building program, though only slightly. In January of 1951, for instance, he had to send a letter to Catholics in Canaan, in the far northeast corner of the state, who were ready to begin constructing a church. "In view of the national emergency which has recently been declared," Ryan wrote, "you shall not go ahead with your plans for new construction . . . or purchase any needed materials." But six months later he gave permission to proceed. His building program moved ahead, and not just in rural areas. New high schools were opened in Bennington, Barre, and Newport. New elementary schools came to Rutland, Swanton, St. Albans, Montpelier, and Fair Haven. The St. Peter's and Christ the King schools in Rutland were enlarged. A new wing was added to De Goesbriand Hospital. A sizable piece of property was purchased adjacent to the Catholic orphanage on Burlington's North Avenue, and new offices were created for the growing Vermont Catholic Charities and Don Bosco School. And the cathedral was given a thorough renovation.

Bishop Ryan bought a huge TV antenna and installed it on the roof of his home near the University of Vermont campus. There he tried to watch football and baseball games from Boston, no doubt seeking to follow the action of the Red Sox and the Boston College Eagles. Marie Collins said the reception was often so poor it seemed impossible to tell, through the electronic snow, just what kind of a game he was trying to see.

Bishop Ryan remained in good health, though often wearing a brace to support his troublesome back, until 1956. He was 76 years old that fall when he developed a bowel obstruction that was found to be cancerous. Surgery was recommended, and on November 2 he walked from his residence to nearby De Goesbriand Hospital to be admitted for the operation. The surgery was expected to be relatively routine, though the bishop had told a close associate that he might not survive. During the operation, the patient began to bleed heavily. Every effort was made to stop the hemorrhage, as panic gripped the operating room. The hospital chaplain was summoned, though the strain of it all become so great that at one point he fled to an open window and vomited. Bishop Ryan bled to death. That night, Cardinal Cushing called the bishop's residence to say he couldn't believe the news of his old friend's death.

Bishop Ryan, who had led the Burlington diocese for 11 years, died on the 57th anniversary of Bishop de Goesbriand's passing. An editorial writer noted:

> The entire episcopate of Bishop Ryan was devoted to fulfilling the accomplishments which Bishop de Goesbriand must

have dreamed about as he struggled and rejoiced in the early formative days of the Diocese of Burlington . . . When Bishop de Goesbriand was commencing his labors in Vermont he had five priests to assist him among a flock of about ten thousand people. The diocese presently numbers two hundred and fourteen priests, secular and religious, and approximately one hundred and sixteen thousand Catholics. The Lord has supplied the increment as His faithful shepherds labored to fulfill His will.

Reminiscences

IN THE COURSE OF RESEARCHING *An Inland See,* groups of Catholics were gathered in seven Vermont communities to discuss their lives in the church. Meetings were held in St. Albans, Rutland, Bennington, Brattleboro, St. Johnsbury, Montpelier, and Newport. The result was the revealing of a considerable amount of history, and the collection of a goodly number of very quotable quotes.

My grandmother was married when she was fourteen. She and my grandfather had 13 kids; they started having kids right away. I grew up in St. Johnsbury; I was born there in 1914. We weren't allowed to speak English at home. We lived in a French neighborhood. In school, we were taught English one hour a week, and most of the brothers couldn't speak English. We went to school, to the brothers. They were tough, strict. But you learned. The Mass was in Latin, the sermon was in French.

Alcide Cote, South Burlington

I grew up in Rochester and we didn't have a church. Sometimes the priest came over from Bethel and said Mass in the G.A.R. hall. In the summer, we drove to Bethel for services. Sometimes we didn't go at all.

Yvonne Sergeant, South Burlington

During the war there were three Masses, and every one was packed. You had to get there early, or you stood up. They wanted their boys to come home.

Alcide Cote, South Burlington

My folks were Catholic Democrats; Aunt Edith and Uncle Fred were Protestant Republicans. In those days, Catholics weren't supposed to eat meat on Friday. My dear aunt, who ran a boardinghouse in Benson, tempered the winds to the shorn lamb on my account. Those poor boarders, though they were all Protestants, might as well have been Catholic when Fridays came round. No meat was served at Aunt Edith's table.

Vincent Naramore, Burlington

Benediction was at four o'clock on Saturday. I'd be hunting squirrels on Dunton's Ledge and I'd look at my watch. Three-thirty. I'd run all the way, hide my rifle somewhere, and go to benediction. Then I'd go back and get the rifle and shoot a couple more squirrels. It was about halfway to Proctor.

Arthur Crowley, Rutland, M.S.J. '45

Monsignor Kennedy, Christ the King, he's practically the history of the east side of Rutland for 50 years. What a force he was. He was the boss. If you had problems, you went to the rectory. His advice was wise. Nothing wishy-washy about that man. He was loved and respected.

Arthur Crowley, Rutland

Msgr. John Brown. He was a financial genius. He knew how to invest, knew the stock market. Rumor has it that he saved the Rutland Royals, the Northern League baseball team, one summer. Also, quietly paid some college tuitions, particularly for those who wanted to be priests.

Arthur Crowley, Rutland

There were two Crowley brothers from Rutland who became priests. Their mother, Mary Crowley, decided they would be priests, and that was that.

Arthur Crowley, Rutland

Father O'Connor, pastor at St. Peter's, he was a saintly man. Everybody loved him. He was on his way to Montreal, going to Rome. A car came over the brow of the hill and hit him head on. Killed him. What a shame.

Arthur Crowley, Rutland

I went to St. Peter's. The nuns were strict, but not too strict. They had to have discipline, the classes were so huge. I can't think of one bad teacher among them.

Arthur Crowley, Rutland

The church leadership is much more humble now. And that is a good thing. The whole idea of the priesthood is to serve people, not to be worshipped by them.

Fr. Wendell Searles, Vicar General

There is a supernatural element to the priesthood. I'm convinced there was some type of calling that came to me that this was where I belonged. I've never looked back.

Fr. Wendell Searles

Monsignor Kennedy was famous for turning out the lights. Dr. Cosgrove came in the church one day shining a flashlight, trying to make a point. It didn't work.

Fr. Reid Mayo, Rutland

I sent out a questionnaire for the 50th reunion of Mount St. Joseph's Academy. "Thanks to the Sisters of St. Joseph" was the most common comment I got.

Carolyn "Connie" Omland, Rutland

Sister M. Baptista . . . She was the most extraordinary teacher I ever had. She taught all of the courses in the freshman class . . . I mean, she was brilliant in any curriculum. Languages, Algebra, English, history . . . Latin and Greek probably, she taught all of that. She could do anything . . . She taught English, she started a dramatic club. She ran it and she was excellent in that. Excellent director. She was a great writer and poet. And she established a library. Used to buy books and all that. She was really an extraordinary person. A magnificent woman.

Paul Guare, Montpelier

Father Crowley, in Woodstock. People loved him. He was brilliant. He had a group of intellectuals who met at the rectory on winter evenings. Vincent Sheehan, the writer, was one of them.

Arthur Crowley, Rutland

I went to M.S.J. right after the Depression. The tuition was $30 a year and we couldn't afford the $30.

Geraldine Young, Rutland

Adam turned to Eve and said, "We live in an age of transition." It's been that way ever since.

Fr. Reid Mayo, Rutland

When I came to M.S.J., I couldn't believe it, the spirit of the fans. Once a Mountie, always a Mountie.

Sister Ann Marshall, Rutland

I remember 1953, we celebrated the 100th anniversary of the diocese. Cardinal Cushing said Mass at the fairground. The grandstand was packed.

Joseph Tilden, Rutland

I was in the first graduating class, 1954, at Immaculate Heart of Mary. The hardworking blue-collar people struggled to build that church.

Elizabeth "Betty" Adamsen, Rutland

The young people aren't going to church every Sunday. But they are making good moral decisions. They are aware and they make socially conscious decisions. The influence of the church is there. I believe they will come back, go to church.

Carolyn "Connie" Omland, Rutland

I was in the sixth grade. The nuns were crying. One of their students had been killed in Europe. It was the first time that the war really came home, that we realized what the war was all about. We had never seen a nun cry before.

Joseph Tilden, Rutland

Father Borland had a special service when President Bush bombed Iraq. The church was packed.

Irene Quirk, Rutland

We have people working for peace, people working in hospice. There are so many ways people can do things today. This is religion in action. It's not just going to church. We are the children of God.

Carolyn "Connie" Omland, Rutland

Sacred Heart Parish began with the Betit family, the LaFlames, LaGrosses, Racicots, Bellemares.

Hector Betit, Bennington

In Wilmington Saturday night was the dance, Sunday morning in the same building was the Mass. It was a wilderness area.

Hector Betit, Bennington

Yes, and they didn't have to go home between.

Paul Caron, Bennington

My mother's cousin was a brother of Brother Andre. Brother Andre would come from Montreal to heal my mother, who was sick. They said he could read your conscience. I didn't want him to read mine. I didn't go near him.

Hector Betit, Bennington

I was sent to a priest at the Sacred Heart to have my ear healed. He kept asking me if I felt any heat. I didn't, but I said I did just to get it over with. But you know, he cured me.

Sister Gertrude Connollay, Bennington

The people of Bennington really fought for a Catholic high school. It lasted for 10 years, then it closed, which is very sad. Father Spinelli was killed in an airplane crash on his way to Montpelier, in the mountains near Rutland. If he hadn't been killed, Bennington Catholic would have lasted. The day he left, I said, "Father, you're not going to fly today." It was hot, hazy, you couldn't see a thing. But he was so excited. We didn't know how much we loved that man until he died.

Sister Gertrude Connollay, Bennington

The day they merged St. Francis de Sales and Sacred Heart nobody knew what was going to happen. Even the bishop was nervous. They met halfway between the churches. They carried flags and banners. It went okay.

Paul Caron, Bennington

Pownal just celebrated their 100th anniversary as a mission. There was a time it looked like it had to close, because of the shortage of priests. But when the women get involved, then things get done.

Sister Gertrude Connollay, Bennington

We still have reunions of Bennington Catholic. After 30 years they still come back. It was a school that was blessed.

Sister Mary Elizabeth Conning, Bennington

I grew up in Rutland. Monsignor Brown, Mother Colomba, Franklin Roosevelt. It seemed like they'd be here forever. When Roosevelt died, we said the Rosary all morning.

Sister Gertrude Connollay, Bennington

Monsignor Rand, he was fabulous. On holy days, we all trooped over from school to church. At the end of Mass, he said, "You've been good so I'll give you the day off." Course, we had it off anyway. He fined you 50 cents if you stepped on the school lawn.

Jean Highter, Brattleboro

My mother thought I was going to be a nun. Then I had seven children. I think I did my duty for God and country.

Dorothy Martino, Brattleboro

The Catholic kids were suspended because they got to school late, when they'd been to Mass. Because of that it was decided to start a Catholic school here, and it opened within months—St. Michael's.

Helen Moynihan, Brattleboro

I had a hard time getting from Guilford here to Brattleboro, to school. They wouldn't let a Catholic ride on the bus. It went right by our front door. I found private transportation and I went anyway.

Robert Franklin, Vernon

Father Murray would be driving back from the hospital and my mother would be walking and he used to stop and say, "I wish I could give you a ride, but people will talk." That was in the 1950s. Thank God times have changed.

Jean Highter, Brattleboro

St. Patrick's Day was the biggest thing. We had entertainment, a dance, it went all day. One little boy, everyone was supposed to have a green cane, and his wasn't so they painted it green and it didn't have time to dry. It got stuck under his arm.

George Parmenter, Brattleboro

There was this Irish housekeeper, late for church. There was this boy sitting on the corner. She was hurrying to church and she asked him, "Is Mass out?" He said, "No, but your slip is showing."

Jean Highter, Brattleboro

Joe Austin told me his father told him he had to walk up the railroad tracks to go to church. The Irish couldn't walk up the street. It was tough for the early Catholics in Brattleboro. It wasn't just Brattleboro, it was everywhere.

Stephen Baker, Brattleboro

What changed it all, the prejudice against Catholics, was World War II. Before the war it was awful. But when you were in a foxhole, everyone was a Christian. Once the war was over and we came home, the intermarriages started. It broke the whole barrier, thank God.

Helen Moynihan, Brattleboro

The Irish came with the railroads, and started our church, in 1863. When the French came, to work in the cotton mill, they wanted their own church. Monsignor Rand said no. So they came to church here. We have always had one church.

George Parmenter, Brattleboro

In 1959, at St. Michael's, what a basketball team we had. We won 24 of 25, and we beat Marian of Barre in the state finals. We only lost one game, to a school in Massachusetts. They beat us down there in an afternoon game. They made us play the first half with the sun coming through the windows in our faces. The second half, it was gone. We beat them easy when they came up here.

Frank Martocci, Brattleboro

The church, Notre Dame des Victoires, burned in 1966. I was up on Maple Street. I thought maybe I was seeing the sun vaporizing moisture on the roof. It was a beautiful sunny morning.

Claude A. Donna, St. Johnsbury

I was standing looking up at the smoke, and I saw the steeple fall. It was such a beautiful church, up on the hill. It was so sad.

Gerald Heon, St. Johnsbury

The Notre Dame priests served all those missions. My grandfather used to take the priests to the lumber camps, up at Stevens Mills. They'd sleep on tables in the cook shacks. They'd go with horse and sleigh. The parishioners chipped in and bought Father Boissonault a heavy coat, he was so cold.

Gerald Heon, St. Johnsbury

The nuns, the teachers, would talk to the girls about becoming nuns. In those days, every family wanted at least one of their children to go into the religious life. There were many prayers sent heavenward for that.

Bernice Payeur, St. Johnsbury

My sister Marie, the nuns were bound and determined she was going to become a nun. But she had her eye on somebody, and he had his eyes on her. The nuns were so disappointed.

Claude Donna, St. Johnsbury

We wore white dresses for First Communion and Confirmation. They were the most beautiful ceremonies. They made me think of the Vatican. Hundreds of people, not just Catholics, would be on the streets to watch.

Ella Ziter, St. Johnsbury

At Notre Dame Church, for Midnight Mass, people would start lining up at 11. The doors didn't open until 11:30.

Cecile Smith, St. Johnsbury

The history of the little parishes of the Northeast Kingdom, in places like Lunenberg and Gilman, is an absolute monument to the faith of the people.

Bernice Payeur, St. Johnsbury

I have three sisters in religion. My father worked at Fairbanks. The men that worked in the foundry would come home at night all black, soot all over their faces. Before that he worked in the woods. He'd tell about the log drives in the spring, putting the logs down the river.

Gerard Chaloux, St. Johnsbury

Monsignor Dane, if he heard you talking English, oh my gosh. He could hear students talking from the rectory window. If he heard them talking English, he'd holler down.

Claude Donna, St. Johnsbury

You couldn't have your arms uncovered in school. You had to put on what they called a manchette, to cover your arms. You had to wear stockings, but during the war you couldn't get stockings so we'd take a pen and draw a line up our legs, to look like stockings.

Cecile Smith, St. Johnsbury

Joe Morin, my step-grandfather, he was quite a talker. He'd come to visit. We knew everything he said was not true. It made good listening, though. One winter he couldn't get his logs out. No snow. He prayed and prayed to Mary. He needed to skid his logs. Then it started snowing and it didn't stop. He said, "I'm going to have to pray again." The snow stopped.

Claude Donna, St. Johnsbury

Joe Morin, he was quite a Joe.

Phil Villeneuve, St. Johnsbury

At Lyndonville, we had a sermon in French and one in English. Father Pontbriand, God love him, he's a legend in Lyndonville. Father Pontbriand was there during the depression and the railroad strike. He had a camp up in Lost Nation. He brought venison down and shared it with his parishioners. He seemed to have an endless supply of venison, bless his heart. He brought fish down, vegetables from his garden. He had this big dog, Tom, who sat beside you at the end of the pew. He was a good Catholic dog.

Rita Morency, St. Johnsbury

Father Fortin got a moose every year. He'd give the parishes meat or hamburgers. My wife went and made hamburger out of the meat.

Stewart Smith, St. Johnsbury

Notre Dame School was closed 26 years. It opened again last fall, 68 pupils. Twenty are from St. Johnsbury and the rest from surrounding towns. There's no discrimination when the state comes to collect your taxes. But they'll only pay tuition to public schools. That's discrimination.

Claude Donna, St. Johnsbury

Father Dwyer. I can see him now with his homburg hat and cigar walking down Main Street. He drove a Pierce Arrow. Wonderful man.

Gerald Heon, St. Johnsbury

I remember Bishop Angell of all the bishops. We've seen more of him. When I visit with him, I feel like I'm visiting with a friend.

Claude Donna, St. Johnsbury

Some of these parishes have had giants. Monsignor Rand in Brattleboro, Monsignor Kennedy in Rutland, Monsignor Dane in St. Johnsbury, for instance.

Msgr. John McSweeney, Burlington

To be a Catholic is not easy.

Frank Gyra, Woodstock

Christ told us there is a life beyond and you're going to be part of it, if you behave yourself. It's that simple.

Frank Gyra, Woodstock

Marshfield, it's a mountain church. I go there once a week. The parishioners take care of the church, clean it, maintain it, run the religious education program. They are wonderful, and I don't think I could do it without them. I come in and say Mass, everything is ready. I think it's as it was in the early history of Vermont. The father is a traveling priest, the parishioners take care of everything.

Fr. Paul Houde, Montpelier

The New York Football Giants trained at St. Michael's College, three summers in the mid-1950s. They were a classy group of people. Vince Lombardi was the offensive coach, Tom Landry the line coach. The head coach was Jim Lee Howells. One day Lombardi had had a difficult day on the field. He went in to take a shower. The dressing facilities were in the basement of the dining hall, pretty primitive. Somebody flushed a toilet or something next door and Lombardi nearly got scalded. He met our athletic director, Doc Jacobs, right after that and started complaining. Doc didn't take anything from anybody and he said, "We win our games on the field, not in the locker room." Lombardi came to his house the next day and apologized.

Edward Markey, South Burlington

Sam Huff was a rookie and he decided he couldn't take any more. He and Don Chandler, the kicker, decided they were going home. They went to the Burlington Airport and Lombardi was sent to bring them back. I saw Huff years later and he confirmed the story. He said, "They didn't give a damn about me, he came to get Chandler." Both men became great players.

Edward Markey, South Burlington

I went to St. Michael's School, up on the hill where the Capital Apartments are now. We went to school to the Sisters of Mercy, very ordered and very structured. I graduated in 1947, 40 of us. There was Sister DePazzi, a wonderful chemistry teacher. She even went to Oak Ridge, Tennessee, to the atomic laboratory, as a consultant.

Patricia Percy, Montpelier

I worked as a nurse at De Goesbriand Hospital. I went there in 1948. We were taught to treat hospital patients like they were hotel guests. The sisters, the Religious Hospitalers of St. Joseph, taught us to treat the whole person, with tender love and care.

Patricia Percy, Montpelier

Our St. Michael's is K through six, but we plan to open a seventh grade in the fall and an eighth grade. We've got a great new principal. Catholic school tends to be a grade or two ahead of public schools because we don't have the discipline problems. Parents like that.

Fr. Paul Houde, Montpelier

The numbers are going up. In any parish that has a school, you'll see the numbers at Mass going up.

Fr. Paul Houde, Montpelier

I have a daughter who goes to church when she pleases. I was sick once, quite sick, and I saw this blond head out in the pew. I said, "Who is this?" It was my daughter.

Donalda Chenette, Berlin

A lot of the shut-ins watch Sister Angelica on the Catholic channel, also the Mass on Sunday morning, on WCAX. We bring them Communion on the first Friday of the month. It means a lot to them.

Fr. Paul Houde, Montpelier

After Vatican II, the Mass became more personal. It opened everything up to the parishioners. It was nice to see the priest turn and face us.

Patricia Percy, Montpelier

I was ordained in 1941 and my first assignment was as chaplain at the De Goesbriand Hospital. The nuns would come in each morning with cookies and milk, I thought they were great. Then I found out that Bishop Brady had told them to build me up, put some weight on me. He was going to send me back to Montreal for postgraduate work.

Msgr. Edwin Buckley, South Burlington

I grew up in Winooski. It wasn't until I was in high school that I realized I was going to a Catholic church. They called it the Irish church. I thought it was just like Anglican or Congregational.

Fr. Maurice Roy, St. Albans

There's two churches here. Was there a rivalry? I guess so, at one time. Father LaVeer and Monsignor Welch wouldn't even talk to each other.

Fr. Leonidas Laroche, St. Albans

I came from Fairfield, with four or five pupils in the school. My parents paid five dollars a week for my room and gave me five dollars a week to eat. I was from one of the first French families in a very Irish town. My grandparents couldn't read or write. I got here in St. Albans, to St. Mary's, and they had flush toilets. We had no plumbing at home. I'd never seen a basketball game.

Henry Raymond, Fairfax

Back in the 1920s Father Gauthier, he had a farm himself. He raised goats. He was instrumental in bringing French families to Highgate to farm. He had his own still in the cellar.

Henry Raymond, Fairfax

The Sheldon church is on the land where there was one of the mineral springs. At one time they were selling so much mineral water up there they couldn't possibly get it all from the springs. They had to be getting it from the river, somewhere. And they were making patent medicines, more alcohol than anything else. But you felt good.

Fr. Bernard Bechard, Sheldon Springs

There was a group of French Canadian priests who bucked the bishop. They were called the Petite Eglise. They would meet in Fairfield. This was in the 1920s. The signatures are still up there in the attic of the rectory. They didn't paint them over.

Fr. Leonidas Laroche, St. Albans

I've gone to St. Anne's Shrine for the last 60 years. My grandfather was a very strong Catholic. When we went we had the novena for nine days before, for somebody sick in the family, or if nothing else for good crops. We didn't go until the middle of July, when the haying was done.

Henry Raymond, Fairfax

We grew up in Winooski. The summer wasn't complete until you went to St. Anne's, that and going to the fair.

Fr. Maurice Roy, St. Albans

The statue of St. Anne, at the shrine. The story is told that they tried to move it inside. It mysteriously moved back outside. That is what they always said. My grandparents sure believed it.

Henry Raymond, Fairfax

I was seven years old when we moved from Quebec to Fairfax. I didn't speak a word of English. I had to learn fast. They thought we were going to hell when we moved to Vermont, because it was in a non-Catholic country. They looked down on us. Now it's not at all the same.

Pat Contois, Newport

Canada's torn down a lot of churches to make parking lots. It's sad, sad.

Paul Major, Newport

Forty-seven young women born in Newport joined the Daughters of Charity.

Norma Major, Newport

Father Clermont built our church. Father Bastien brought him back when he was old. He used to walk over to the church and pray. He never said a Mass in the church. The bishop wouldn't let him.

Patricia Cheney, Newport

Florence Lamothe played the organ in our church for 52 years. I've been in the choir since '44, except two years in the service. Sister Edmund, she was the choir director when I came here. Still is.

Norman Rivard, Newport

It wasn't just Father Clermont who built this huge church, it was the parishioners. My father was a stonecutter. He worked on the church four months and never got a cent of pay. They wanted their church.

Patricia Cheney, Newport

The nuns brought up my mother. They had a big boarding school, right on this hill, next to the church. They had over 365 boarding students. The nuns wanted a chapel and built it without Bishop Rice's permission. Mass was never said there, until he died.

Patricia Cheney, Newport

I taught at Sacred Heart here. My mother worked in the rectory. She worked until she was 90, until she started having strokes. She said she wasn't going to take care of any more priests.

Jeanne Contois, Newport

The church roof had leaked. You could see places where it had stained. There were pigeon stains. It badly needed doing over. I was running bingo for the church at the time. We said, "How are we going to renovate the church?" Father LaFlamme did the fancy painting work. He convinced everyone we could do it. We did.

Dan Bullis, Newport

There isn't a place in this city you can't see our church. To me it means a lot. You sit there every Mass and you say, "I painted that wall, over there. A friend of my grandfather helped build this." Once you work on it, it's yours.

Jeanne Contois, Newport

There used to be five Masses here in Newport. My father worked on the railroad. When the railroad died, Newport died. So did Island Pond.

Patricia Cheney, Newport

I went to St. Mary's Academy in Island Pond, 12 grades in one building. We had the sisters from Maine. I didn't pay one cent of tuition my four years of high school.

Paul Major, Newport

My grandmother said they had kitchen junkets in their homes to raise money to build the church. They wore out the linoleum.

Patricia Cheney, Newport

Father Rouelle wasn't afraid of anything. They took Bishop Angell for a ride up the lake, way up to St. Benoit du Lac. The weather changed, they were lucky to get back. We almost lost the bishop.

Norman Rivard, Newport

We worked so hard to keep our high school going, Sacred Heart. My daughter was in the last graduating class, 1988. It was so sad. If we could have a Catholic high school here now, it would be packed. The hope is still there.

Norma Rivard, Newport

I imagine that the new millennium will bring a lot of people back. It will be a time of coming together.

Sister Ann Marshall, Rutland

CHAPTER

7

THE DEATH OF BISHOP RYAN would bring to the office of bishop of Burlington one of the major figures in the history of Catholicism in the state. But the selection process was somewhat convoluted, and not without considerable drama—perhaps a bit of intrigue. During the last years of Bishop Ryan's episcopate, it had been widely believed in Vermont that the elderly prelate was determined that the talented Msgr. Bernard Flanagan, a Proctor native who had served both Brady and Ryan as diocesan chancellor, would be his successor. But in 1953, Flanagan was suddenly named the first bishop of Norwich, Connecticut. The favorite son was out of the picture.

A year later, in 1954, another Proctor native and the pastor of St. Peter's in Rutland, Robert F. Joyce, was consecrated auxiliary bishop of

Bishops Ryan and Joyce on the occasion of
Bishop Joyce's consecration as auxiliary bishop.

Burlington. The appointment came as something of a surprise. Joyce had been on the list of three priests recommended to Rome for the position by Bishop Ryan, but had been ranked number three. How did the Rutland priest end up the choice of the Vatican? Nobody today seems just sure how it happened. But there is speculation that Francis Cardinal Spellman, of New York, may have had a hand. Perhaps no Catholic in the history of Vermont ever had more friends than "Pat" Joyce, and during his World War II service, as chaplain of a 2,000 bed army hospital in England, Joyce had made the acquaintance of the powerful New York prelate. There was, apparently, considerable surprise in Vermont with Rome's choice of Joyce, and it showed through a little more than two years later when the Vatican determined that Joyce should become the sixth bishop of Burlington. Upon the death of Ryan, the consultors of the diocese had met to choose a diocesan administrator and elected not the only bishop in Vermont, Robert Joyce, but the popular and senior priest Rt. Rev. William Crosby, of Montpelier. So for a short time, Bishop Joyce in Rutland had to acknowledge a monsignor in Burlington as his superior. But not for long. In less than two months, five days before Christmas in 1956, Joyce was appointed bishop of Burlington.

In the entryway of the graceful, marble St. Dominic's Church in Proctor is a marble tablet that lists the names of 21 sons and daughters of Proctor who chose the religious life. At the top is the name of Robert F. Joyce. Also named there is Msgr. Francis Flanagan, long a priest in southern Vermont, who observed in 1998 of his hometown, "The faith sparkled there." Most of the Proctor people who became priests or nuns grew up on West Street, now affectionately known as Pope's Row, the home of many Irish immigrant families who labored in the local marble quarries. But Robert Joyce was raised on another street, across the creek, because his father was in management, working as a foreman at the Vermont Marble Company's machine shop. In an interview conducted in 1969 at the University of Vermont, Joyce recalled, "My father, all his life, had a very pronounced Scotch brogue. He was born in Greenock, on the Clyde, just outside Glasgow in Scotland . . . My mother was born here in Vermont, but her father and mother left Ireland at the time of the potato famine, about the middle of the last century."

"With his father having come from Glasgow," said historian Tom Bassett in 1998, "he would have been naturally tolerant of Protestants. They lived in Proctor and his father was a machinist for Vermont Marble. Pat Joyce was the first boy in the family to go to college." Joyce chose for his college the state university at Burlington, and there a friend, Joseph Johnson from Springfield (who would later serve as governor of Vermont), nicknamed him Pat.

Bishop Joyce and Fr. Louis Gelineau.

Perhaps nobody knew Pat Joyce any better than Bp. Louis Gelineau, for 25 years bishop of Providence, Rhode Island, who as a younger priest served Joyce for many years as chancellor of the Diocese of Burlington and resided with him at the bishop's residence in Burlington. Indeed, many people referred to Father Gelineau and Bishop Joyce, so often seen together, as "Joyce and Rejoice." On a mild winter day in Providence, not long before Christmas, 1998, Bishop Gelineau recalled his longtime superior and close friend. "He came from good Irish stock," said Gelineau. "If you know Proctor, you know those people brought their faith with them. He never went to Catholic school until the seminary. Bishop Rice wondered why a UVM student (he was class of 1917) wanted to be a priest." According to Gelineau, Rice approved of Joyce's attending a seminary in Montreal but, suspicious of his Protestant upbringing in public schools and his schooling at a Yankee university, insisted that Joyce spend an extra two years at the seminary. "He basically said, okay, we'll start you off in Montreal, but you've got to redo your philosophy," Gelineau said. "Bishop Joyce was very strict when it came to religion. He believed that we do what the church allows, we don't do what the church does not allow. He loved the very strict training he received in Montreal. He had a great sense of morality, of right and wrong. It carried him through all of his long life." Gelineau continued, "Later he would be a trustee of UVM. That was unheard of for a Catholic bishop. But he knew so

Fathers Tennien, Joyce, and Brennan.

many people up there. At UVM when he was a student, he was always known as Pat, to hundreds of people he was always Pat."

Joyce was ordained in May of 1923 at the cathedral in Burlington by Bishop Rice. He served in parishes in Brattleboro, Bennington, and Manchester before being named principal of Cathedral High School in Burlington, a post he held for five years. In 1932, he was appointed pastor of St. John Parish in Northfield, where he served for a dozen years. According to Gelineau, "While in Northfield, he got involved in Norwich University. He became a friend of the college president, Gen. Ernest Harmon. He used to tell me years later that when he was bishop, the general would come to see him and would say, before he went up to his office, 'Pray for me while I'm up there. Please may I watch my language while I'm with the bishop.' "

Certainly the general and the bishop shared common experiences on which to base conversation. Joyce had become a military chaplain in 1942 when he volunteered for the army. "He loved the military life," according to Gelineau. "After he came out he was very military. And he got to know everybody in his company. Years later, he was still sending Christmas cards to men who were brought there as patients." While in the military, he also got to know Cardinal Spellman.

After the war, Joyce was assigned to St. Peter's in Rutland and, said Gelineau, "he ran it like the army. His assistant priests thought they were in the army." Soon the

Father Joyce in World War II uniform.

BURLINGTON COMMUNITY LIBRARY
SO BURLINGTON VT

Rutland priest's considerable abili-
ties were becoming recognized statewide. He was elected to the board
of trustees of the University of Vermont and readily accepted, though,
according to Gelineau, "It was unheard of for a priest to become a
trustee of a very Yankee university
such as UVM." Joyce quickly became one of the more active and
outspoken members of the board.

In the early spring of 1952, a
University of Vermont research sci-
entist, Dr. Alex Novikoff, was summoned to Washington to answer
questions concerning his former association with the Communist
Party. It was the height of the
McCarthy era, as Republican U.S.
Sen. Joseph McCarthy, of Wiscon-
sin, was seeking to root out American "Reds." In Washington,
Novikoff refused to answer some of
the questions put to him, pleading
the Constitution's Fifth Amendment

*Bishop Joyce and Archbishop Cushing
on the occasion of Joyce's installation
as bishop of Burlington.*

protection against self-incrimination. Returning home to Burlington, Novikoff
faced severe scrutiny from the university and its president, Carl Borgmann,
who was spurred on by Vermont Gov. Lee Emerson, an ex-officio trustee.
Borgmann launched an inquiry into Novikoff's background and named a
six-person faculty/trustee investigatory committee to determine whether
Novikoff should continue to be a member of the university faculty. The college president chose trustee Joyce to chair the committee. In an interview
many years later, Joyce expressed the opinion that he may have been chosen
with the belief that he would be "tough on Communism" based on the Catholic Church's strong stand against Communism. If that was what the university was after, it didn't get it from Pat Joyce.

The committee held hearings, calling several witnesses including Novikoff
himself. By a vote of five to one, with the chair voting in the majority, the
committee recommended that Dr. Novikoff be retained in his teaching position. But the matter was far from settled. The UVM trustees, heeding the gov-

St. Anne's Shrine.

ernor, voted to ask Novikoff to return to Washington and, this time, answer all the questions. He refused. Novikoff was suspended from the university without pay. The matter raged on for months and became a major story in the Vermont press. It finally came down to a vote of the university trustees as to whether the suspension should be made permanent. The vote was overwhelmingly against Novikoff. Indeed, the only vote in his favor was cast by Father Joyce, who stood firm in his belief that an outrage was being perpetrated.

Novikoff left UVM for Albert Einstein College in New York, where he became a cancer researcher of international importance, once being nominated for a Nobel Prize. During the agonizing deliberations in Burlington, Joyce and Novikoff had struck up an acquaintance. In subsequent years they became friends, and Novikoff was in the audience, at Joyce's invitation, when Joyce was consecrated as a bishop and again when he was made bishop of Burlington. In the spring of 1983, UVM finally took a major step in redressing its wrongs against Dr. Novikoff by awarding him an honorary degree at commencement exercises. Bishop Joyce was among the 6,000 people in attendance at Centennial Field, most of whom rose to give the researcher a prolonged ovation. A year later, Novikoff was invited back to UVM for an oral-history interview about the troubled times three decades earlier. The transcript, preserved at the university, begins with Novikoff's recollection of being present at the two Catholic ceremonies:

Each time he rose, two times at least, he invited me . . . and each time we came and sat in the same pew as Carl Borgmann, and I have had the closest relation with Joyce . . . One of the most, for me, moving portions of the commencement was the meeting we (my family) had with Father Joyce . . . We had this marvelous discussion and it was a most moving thing. So, and of course, he was at that commencement dinner and of course at commencement, you know . . . I didn't have tears in my eyes as now.

Joyce's rise to statewide prominence was well under way before the Novikoff case. In 1953, he was selected to mediate of the contentious Rutland Railroad strike. Joyce performed his difficult tasks well.

It came as a considerable surprise in 1954 when Father Joyce was appointed a bishop, leapfrogging many more senior Vermont priests. Two years later, Bishop Ryan died and Monsignor Crosby was elected to the position of diocesan administrator. Gelineau recalled, "The apostolic delegate in Washington wondered if there a problem with Joyce. He inquired, and found that Bishop Joyce would be just fine as a successor to Ryan." Bishop Ryan had died in November 1956, and Bishop Joyce was chosen just before Christmas. Gelineau: "He brought a military background, tremendous orderliness, to Burlington. His motto was, '*Ut Vitam Habeant,* That they may have life.'" Gelineau recalled that the bishop started writing a newspaper column, for

Blessing of bicycles, Montpelier — April 9, 1960.

the *Vermont Catholic Tribune,* which he titled with his motto. Every column—and he wrote hundreds—ended with the words "that they may have life." Gelineau said, "He'd be driving, he had only one good eye from birth, and he kept a pad of paper beside him. He'd think of something for that column and he'd look down to write something and the car would swerve." In retirement, Joyce collected the best of his columns into a book, *Thoughts to Ponder.* In the foreword he wrote, "Our Lord said: 'I have come that they may have life, and have it more abundantly.' I believed always that He meant life on earth as well as in heaven, and that His mission, and that of His church, encompassed both. Shortly after becoming Bishop of Burlington in 1957, I began writing a brief article each week . . . It was meant to fulfill, in some measure, Christ's command to preach and teach his gospel, leaving to Him the fruit of the work." Joyce's successor as bishop of Burlington, John Marshall, in writing an introduction for the book, commented, "A noted humorist has observed, 'I'd rather see a sermon than hear one any day; I'd rather one would walk with me than merely tell the way.' Bishop Joyce has walked with us along the highways and byways of every town and hamlet of Vermont."

Gelineau recalled, "He was a member of the 251 Club. He claimed he'd been to every town in the state, to the town clerk's office of every town that had one. He'd even been to the remote towns you had to walk into. He loved Vermont. I'd be driving him around the state and he'd say, 'Louis, turn here. I know some people down there.' There was as good a chance that they'd be Protestants as Catholics." Historian Tom Bassett observed in 1998, "Pat Joyce had impeccable credentials as a Vermonter."

Ever on the road, the bishop was always dropping in on local priests, most interested in knowing how they were running their parishes and whether they were getting out to meet the people. Upon entering a town, the bishop would sometimes take note of some name on a mailbox and inquire of the priest if he had paid them a visit. More than once, the bishop had already stopped at a home himself and found that a priest had not been by. He would upbraid the local pastor, particularly if he tried to intimate that a visit had, indeed, been made. Gelineau remembered, "He made the priests take a very detailed census of the parishes. How many kids did they have? Did they go to church? Is the marriage valid? He would look at census cards in the parish and inquire, at random, about names. On the way into Wilmington one day he saw a name on a mailbox and asked Fr. Robert Powers about them. Fr. Powers knew nothing of them, and ever after he would talk about 'that damn mailbox.' "

Before becoming bishop of Burlington, Joyce had been an avid golfer, a left-hander who played only with irons. But because of his relentless approach to his new job, he gave up golf. He did not sacrifice his other beloved game—bridge. "He lived at 52 Williams Street from 1957–72," Gelineau said, "and he had people in for bridge all the time, for bridge in the afternoon, then dinner, and bridge in the evening. He was a great bridge player. He did the *New York Times* Bridge Challenge every day. Incidentally, he read the *Burlington Free Press* in the morning, the *Rutland Herald* at lunch, and the *Times* in the evening. Many of the people who played bridge with him were life masters, and he tried to be better than they were. He hated to lose and he would go over the games at breakfast. Sometimes I would fill in and I hated it, the pressure."

Gelineau continued, "He was a great walker and he kept in good health. He liked music and he always subscribed to the UVM concert series, the Lane Series. He loved Broadway musicals. One night he went to Hello, Dolly! with Dorothy Lamour, and he was sitting there in his full regalia and she walked out on the ramp and she gave him a big wink as she went by. He loved it. He'd quote from Broadway songs in his talks, things like 'climb every mountain, ford every stream.' He had a favorite, and some people got sick of hearing it:

Bishop Joyce leaving for Vatican Council II.

No bell is a bell 'til you ring it.
No song is a song 'til you sing it.
The love in your heart wasn't put there to stay.
Love isn't love 'til you give it away.

"In retirement, he'd quote the 'September Song,' 'It's a long long time, from May to December. But the days grow shorter when you reach September.'"

Everywhere the bishop went, he met more and more Vermonters. Joyce had a remarkable memory, and would greet people throughout the state with their full names. He compiled a card file of his friends that eventually contained hundreds and hundreds of entries. Everyone got a card at Christmas, a formidable administrative task. And cards came at other times until one associate recalled, "It seemed like he sent thank-you cards to thank-you cards." Joyce wrote countless letters and was always on the phone.

He took a break from his arduous duties each winter, driving to Florida for a vacation. "He went to Lake Worth, for one month. The people down there said their social life didn't began until Bishop Joyce got there."

During Joyce's years as bishop of Burlington, great changes in the Catholic Church occurred worldwide. For perhaps a quarter century there had been agitation for major change within the church, for reform. But the man at the helm, Pope Pius XII, was not a man for whom change came easily. The pope died in the fall of 1958 and the cardinals, assembled at the Vatican, promptly elected an elderly, amiable cardinal from Venice who, it was apparently felt, would be a fine caretaker for the short time he would serve as holy father. But Angelo Giuseppe Cardinal Roncalli, who took the name of John XXIII, would be anything but a caretaker. In the words of Frank Gyra of Woodstock, a lifelong Catholic and a keen observer of his church, "It took a little old cardinal from up in Venice to turn the whole church upside down." The new pope declared there was a need "to open the window and let fresh air in." Thus he summoned to Rome all the church's hierarchy, its bishops and cardinals, for a thorough discussion of the need for change in the church.

Vatican II, as it was called, began in October 1962 with Bishop Joyce in attendance, one of 2,540 churchmen present. The historic gathering at St. Peter's would last more than three years, and Joyce took pride in the fact that he attended all the sessions. According to Gelineau, "He said later that being bishop at the time of Vatican II was the one great thrill of his life." Many years later, Dr. Carlyle Adams, a friend, who was also at the council, described Joyce's long stay in Rome:

> Afternoons, when the council was not in session, the
> bishop of Burlington would read, study the documents, in

preparation for the next session, write letters and his weekly article for the Burlington diocesan newspaper. All his writing was done by hand. In the morning, after he celebrated mass in the hotel chapel, he would take a stroll and greet all the shopkeepers. He always spoke Italian, with a very marked Yankee accent . . . Then he would don his episcopal vestments and walk over to St. Peter's Basilica—he did not use the bus that was sent to pick up the bishops. At twilight, he could be seen strolling across St. Peter's Square on the way to the post office to drop off the results of the day's writing. He stands out in any crowd because he is tall and erect, with snow-white hair. He marches like a soldier, but he sees everyone he passes.

During his time in Rome, the bishop kept up a regular correspondence with Monsignor Gelineau, keeping abreast of even the most minute details of goings-on back in Vermont and issuing countless orders for conducting the affairs of the diocese. He also reported regularly on events of the council, in letters both to Gelineau and to the diocese, sent from Joyce's home away from home, the Hotel Michelangelo in Rome:

October 24, 1962
The Council is very interesting. An 82 year old Jesuit Bp. died this A. M. on the steps of St. Peter's—an ideal place to meet the Good Lord . . . My love to all in our House. Living in Rome is not like living at 52 Williams, interesting and varied though it is.

November 18, 1962
The atmosphere is distinctly spiritual, like a retreat, and the many differences of opinion are expressed as various approaches to a common end . . . Any bishop may put his name in to speak for a maximum of ten minutes, or he may write his comments for submission to the Secretariat and the proper Commission . . . The public address system is excellent and gradually one's Latin improves with daily hearing . . . Everybody indicates great pastoral concern and a desire for the Church to face the problems of our age, and meet the needs of the people. Naturally there are those of conservative and of more liberal minds, but there are no clear-cut lines, and no obvious forming of parties or blocs. I

believe, however, that a majority of the Bishops are what might be called on the liberal or progressive side, in that they are ready for changes in practices and attitudes that will make the Church more acceptable to the faithful and those outside the fold.

AUTHOR'S NOTE: The work of the council was suspended on June 3, 1963, when Pope John died. A second session of the Council convened on September 29, after the selection of Pope Paul VI. Bishop Joyce wrote:

[Undated]

Pope John XXIII said that the calling of the Council was a sudden inspiration of the Holy Spirit without previous thought on his part. Pope Paul VI seemed to expand and amplify the purpose of the Council in his strong opening address on September 29, and to emphasize two trends that had become evident at the first session in 1962, and to make them paramount. The bringing together of all Christians in unity has now become a primary goal, rather than the result of updating the Church itself; and the second prime purpose is the building of a bridge to the contemporary world, that the redemptive work of Christ may reach all men on the religious, human and cultural plane.

November, 1963

Rare are days in the Council when moving and touching things occur, which stir the more than 2,000 Bishops and several hundred experts, observers, and lay auditors. One of them recently was the occasion when Archbishop Josyf Slipyi, of the Ukraine in Russian, who was recently released after 18 years imprisonment by the Communists, rose to speak. Applause is rare in St. Peter's, since it is against the rules of procedure, but he was greeted with spontaneous and prolonged applause as a modern day confessor of the faith and living martyr. He gave a stirring address indicating that his spirit had not been broken by his years of confinement and suffering, and his face shows a man of interior serenity and patience.

On November 26, 1963, in Burlington, Monsignor Gelineau sent the following telegram at the behest of Joyce in Rome:

Mrs. Jacqueline Kennedy
Washington, D.C.

Dear Mrs. Kennedy:
The Right Reverend Patrick C. Brennan, P.A., Vicar General of the Diocese of Burlington, has asked me to express to you and to the family of the late President the most sincere sympathy of the clergy and faithful of the Diocese of Burlington on the occasion of the death of our beloved President.

We feel that you will take comfort in knowing that his Excellency, the Most Reverend Robert F. Joyce, D.D., Bishop of Burlington, cabled this office from the Ecumenical Council in Rome that Requiem Masses should be celebrated in every church of the diocese for the repose of the soul of President Kennedy and for God's blessings upon his loved ones and the nation in this time of great loss. These Requiem Masses will be offered on November 25.

Please be assured of our continued prayers for the intentions for which the world has prayed so fervently during these past few days.

Sincerely yours in Christ,
Very Rev. Msgr. Louis E. Gelineau, Chancellor

The fourth and final session of the council opened in late September 1965. Joyce wrote:

November 5, 1965

We have just come from one of the great days of the Council when the first solemn vote on five complete Constitutions was taken, the Holy Father added his vote of approval, and the five were publicly and officially proclaimed as Council documents . . . The Holy Father entered St. Peter's in solemn procession, accompanied by the Cardinals and many Vatican officials, and surrounded by the 20 concelebrants chosen from various parts of the world to concelebrate the Mass with the Pope. St. Peter's echoed with the famous hymn Tu es Petrus (thou art Peter) . . . The final ceremony included the announcing of the results of the votes, the formal approval by Pope Paul, and the official promulgation of the five Constitutions. The Holy Father addressed the Council

Bishop Joyce at the council.

with unusual eloquence and feeling and his address was most warmly received.

December 3, 1965

The fundamental point, overlooked by many writers, commentators, and readers, is that the Church cannot change the divine law or modify revealed truth. These have come from above; the church holds them in trust by Christ's commission. The world would like to take these things in its own hands, and make them over to suit its convenience and pleasure; and some in the world want the Council to do this. Its function is to reform, renew, restore, verify, to conform itself and the world to Christ's teachings and the divine law . . .

December, 1965

The Council cannot perform the miracle of changing human nature, and of curing all the ills which beset the world. Some will be frightened and shaken by what they think are radical innovations, which they are not, actually; others will be disappointed that every abuse or custom is not abolished at one fell swoop, that every teaching does not become completely clear, that every human problem is not offered an immediate and easy remedy. The fruits of the

Council are and will be immeasurable, but there will still be questions unanswered and problems unsolved. We creatures were not made Gods, and we shall never have the wisdom and power of God on this earth; we do have the priceless consolation of knowing that the Holy Spirit has been promised and given to the Church to guide her and her children.

The council adjourned, and Bishop Joyce was home before Christmas, 1965. Despite his assurances that change would not be radical, conforming to the new rules drafted by Vatican II proved a considerable challenge. Change came to the Catholic Church in Vermont as at no other time in its history. Just before Christmas, 1965, Bishop Joyce granted an interview to the *Burlington Free Press*. "The real purpose of the Council, as Pope John envisioned it, was to make renewal, reform, and to update," he said. "All organizations made up of human beings need this thing constantly and all other results of the Council are really products of this renewal and self-study." Joyce said that some effects of Vatican II would become readily apparent, while years would pass before others would take effect. Despite the reassuring words, Joyce saw to it that no American diocese instituted change any faster than Burlington. Bishop Gelineau, in 1998, said, "He had been thrilled all along by Vatican II, by the chance to go. When changes came, he said, 'This is what the church wants, we're going to see they are done.' Later, he lamented that Vatican II went in some ways too far. He became a taskmaster about the liturgy. People were doing a great deal of experimenting, using texts that were not allowed, for instance. The bishop issued newsletters to the priests saying things like, 'I hear this is being done. This is not allowed.'"

Much later in life, Joyce looked back on the time of change and said, "All the things which the Vatican Council recommended I had to establish. That included everything from turning the altars around to the vernacular, priests' senate, sisters' senate, and parish councils in every parish. I call myself a liberal in that measure. I am, however, strongly against changing anything that the church does not recommend."

Change came, as the following headlines that appeared in the *Vermont Catholic Tribune* make clear:

Dec. 13, 1963:	Commission on Church Unity Envisioned by Bishop Joyce
Feb. 14, 1964:	Bishop Announces Liturgy Changes Effective Sunday
Sept. 14, 1964:	Changes in Liturgy Only Beginning
Oct. 23, 1964:	English Mass Begins November 29

Jan. 9, 1965:	Non-Latin Mass Well Received in Vermont, Says Bishop
Sept. 5, 1965:	Bishop Joyce Celebrates First TV Mass in Vermont
Jan. 21, 1966:	Vermont Clergy, Religious, Laity to Be Elected to Form Historic New Pastoral Commission
March 3, 1967:	Sixteen Elected to Posts in Diocese Priests' Senate
May 12, 1967:	Liturgy Changes: English Approved in Canon of Mass
Sept. 8, 1967:	Burlington Diocese Becomes Third in U.S. to Receive Saturday Mass O.K.
Sept. 19, 1967:	First Meeting of Sisters' Senate
Sept. 22, 1967:	Funeral Liturgy Changes: Experiment Begins
Oct. 27, 1967:	Major Ecumenical Move: Three Priests to Vermont Council of Churches Meet
Feb. 15, 1969:	Traveling Workshops Throughout State: New Liturgy Explained
March 26, 1969:	Women Earn Larger Role in Certain Circumstances
July 28, 1970:	Catholic Church to Tell Finances for First Time
Nov. 18, 1970:	Official: Bishop Joyce Issues Liturgy Guidelines
Nov. 25, 1970:	Important Step in the Religious History of Vermont: The Diocese of Burlington Was Warmly Received into Affiliate Membership by the Vermont Ecumenical Council and Bible Society at Its First Meeting Saturday in Montpelier

As Father Tennien had done years earlier, altars were moved forward, and as Tennien had tried but failed to win permission to do, the priest faced the congregation to say Mass. The ancient ban on eating meat on Friday was ended. "In Vatican II, appearances changed. There were not a lot of fundamental changes," according to Vincent Naramore. "It was not that difficult to adjust." Msgr. Francis Flanagan recalled, "I welcomed all of the changes. There was no real substantial change. But some clerics took it as license and some silly stuff went on."

In 1973, a history of Newport's St. Mary Star of the Sea parish was published, and it summed up the times of change:

> The day of statuary has passed into time; gone are the statues of St. Anthony, St. Theresa of Lisieux and others which formerly occupied the sanctuary and transept altars. The statues of the Blessed Virgin, Sacred Heart of Jesus, St. Joseph and Ste. Anne remain as does the artistry of Mr. Rochon; gone are the copes of gold; the huge black cata-

falque which for over fifty years surrounded the body of the deceased with lighted candles on all four sides and above the casket. No longer do the altar boys have to light 60 or 70 candles of the catafalque prior to each funeral. The monstrance of gold in the center of which reposed the Blessed Sacrament surrounded by rays of gold similar to rays of

Bishop Joyce at his desk on South Williams Street in Burlington.

the sun is rarely used. Many recall the beauty of the ceremonies during which the monstrance was elevated in solemn benediction or stood on the main altar enshrining the Blessed Sacrament during forty-hour devotions. There have been, as must be expected, changes in the manner and method of expressing our recognition of and dependence upon Almighty God. As we approach the coming century the faith of our fathers remains undimmed . . .

In 1998, two Brattleboro women, both parishioners of St. Michael's Church, looked back on that time. Jean Highter said, "I remember all the meetings. People couldn't accept this from their personal feelings. What do you mean do it this way? You mean I've done it wrong all these years? It was hard. It divided people into little camps." Karen Golden said, "A lot of our treasures were just thrown out. The church was stripped, the church was bare. We all know you don't worship a statue, but when you're raising children, teaching about Jesus, you need statues. But it was exciting. Vatican II was like a shot of adrenaline. It made you think of the church in terms beyond Brattleboro, beyond Vermont. It made you think of the world."

There was another offshoot to the liberalization of the church. Ed Hurley, a lifelong member of the same Brattleboro church, said in 1998, "We went through some terrible times in this parish. Seven priests left this parish, but we're still alive." In 1999, Father Searles, diocesan vicar general, said of those times, "We lost some good priests. For a time, they were leaving in droves."

Fr. Reid Mayo, of Rutland's Christ the King Church, said: "We were lucky as a church, that we had a pope who said, 'Let's get together and see how we can do this better.' Everything was changing. All institutions went through a crisis of some kind at that time. The church was ready to meet the crisis. Most institutions were not. It was divine leadership, the vision of John XXIII. If he hadn't anticipated it, it all would have collapsed around us."

Those years were times of turmoil. In 1964, the limited conflict in Vietnam escalated to a full-blown war when Pres. Lyndon Johnson pushed the Tonkin Gulf Resolution through Congress. American military might poured into Southeast Asia. At home, campuses rebelled, and many Americans took to the streets calling for a peace. On March 29, 1968, even the old soldier Bishop Joyce was admitting concern about the still-growing war; that day the bishop allowed Vermont priests to give counsel, through the Vermont Council of Churches, to young men receiving draft notices.

Work at 52 South Williams Street seldom stopped. Bishop Joyce labored noon and night, adhering to a strict schedule. An associate recalled, "He got up at the same time, ate lunch at the same time. He'd have a nap right after lunch and God forgive anyone who woke him up. Then he'd go on working, sometimes far into the night." Sometimes, the bishop would write penciled instructions on pieces of yellow notepaper and toss them from his second-floor office down the stairwell, to be picked up and obeyed. The messages came to be known as "notes from God." Joyce was a stern taskmaster, and his heavy-handed leadership grated on many priests. He strongly favored ecumenism. When Pat Joyce attended a Protestant funeral and walked down the aisle of a Protestant church escorting a grieving Protestant widow, a complaint went even to Rome. The bishop was undaunted.

Late in his life, Joyce, the former principal of Cathedral High School, was asked about the value of a Catholic education. He said, "Education involves all of life, so when religious ideals are excluded, an important element is omitted. Likewise, with moral principles, about which people differ, it is difficult in public schools to go beyond the most fundamental points which people are willing to accept."

During Joyce's tenure, Catholic school enrollment in Vermont reached its peak. That occurred in 1959, when 14,309 students were studying in diocesan graded and secondary schools. Fr. Wendell Searles, diocesan vicar general and a former high school principal himself, looked back on that time in a 1999 interview. "We had 10 high schools, and 27 grade schools," he said. "Then it began to fall. The Swart Case in South Burlington was important. Up until 1961, towns that didn't have high schools paid tuition to Catholic schools if they so chose. That case in 1961 made it unconstitutional for towns to pay tuition to Catholic schools. Up to that point, tuition was very minimal. Sisters staffed the schools and got only a very small stipend. The parishes supported the schools. Once we lost town tuition payments, our tuitions began to rise."

At the same time, the number of sisters in Vermont religious orders was declining. Thus the number of low-cost teachers available for Catholic schools declined. Searles said, "Our costs went up. We had to bring in more laypeople to teach. Enrollment went down. The more you charge, the less they come. I went to Rice High School as principal in 1966 and we had 32 sisters and four priests. Today there are three sisters and one priest on half-time, as a teacher."

Alarmed at the decline in teachers and enrollments in diocesan schools, in 1967 Bishop Joyce appointed a task force, chaired by John Donaghue of Burlington, to study Catholic education in Vermont. Three months later, Donaghue released what he called its "chilling" findings. Without state help, a dim future was predicted for Catholic education, with the likely result of a substantially increasing burden on Vermont public schools faced with taking in more and more Catholic students. Bishop Joyce, days before the report was released, met with Gov. Deane C. Davis and asked for state aid for Catholic schools. Davis was sympathetic, but the effort died aborning in the General Assembly. Catholic school closings accelerated. Elizabeth Franklin of Vernon was a student at St. Michael's High School in nearby Brattleboro

St. Mary's parochial school, Middlebury.

when that school shut down. "It closed in 1968," she recalled. "We were upset. The Sisters of St. Joseph taught us, the education was wonderful. It was a sad, sad time."

By 1972, Joyce's last year as bishop, Catholic school enrollment had dropped by nearly two-thirds from its peak, 13 years earlier, to just 5,221. The number of schools had dropped from 37 to 19. A Berlin woman, Donalda Chenette, remembered the closing of her high school: "St. Michael's, in Montpelier, closed in 1967. It had been rumored for years. We all went to a meeting and stood in the back and listened to them close our school. A lot of black suits were there. So I graduated from the local high school. I had a chip on my shoulder at the public school. The teachers were out the door before we were. You didn't see that at St. Michael's."

The bishop chose to confront other serious matters. Holding a unique position with his many ties statewide, particularly to the state university, Joyce let it be known in 1956 that he was much concerned about the future of hospitals in the Burlington area. The two big hospitals, Catholic De Goesbriand and Mary Fletcher Hospital, were competing for patients and offering many duplicate services. Both were struggling to keep with up the advance of modern technology through the purchase of expensive new high-tech equipment. Approved nursing schools were operating in both hospitals, as were emergency departments, radiology, maternity, and psychiatry departments. Joyce believed that a merger of the two facilities would be in the long-term best interests of both, a merger that also should include the UVM College of Medicine. Certainly the fact that the De Goesbriand Hospital was deeply in debt weighed heavily on Joyce's mind. In the spring of 1957, a joint committee made up of representatives of the two hospitals and the medical school sat down in Burlington to discuss the future.

Feelings ran high. The De Goesbriand Hospital enjoyed deep loyalty from Vermont Catholics. Joyce was later to write, "There is always an unfair amount of nostalgia when a traditional identity is lost, but I believe the merger has been beneficial to the entire community, as well as to the university and the two hospitals." That merger finally came to pass just before Christmas in 1966, when the boards of the two hospitals became one. Thus the Medical Center Hospital of Vermont was created. In 1972, the De Goesbriand Hospital building became the home of the newly incorporated University Health Center.

As the General Assembly convened in early January of 1970, legislation greatly liberalizing the state's abortion laws was immediately introduced. The House Judiciary Committee held an emotional hearing in the well of the House on a January night in 1970. Bishop Joyce did not attend, but sent a statement to be read on his behalf:

> In the strongest possible terms I want to express my opposition to the legislative proposals regarding abortion. There are those who would like to make it appear that anti-abortion principles are those of a small religious minority. Actually such principles are held and advocated by people of many religious denominations, and of none, motivated by human and moral implications of abortion . . . I hope Vermont legislators will refuse to liberalize the laws on abortion, and that our citizens will oppose such changes. Emphasis is placed on rare cases which have a sentimental appeal, but always is involved the destruction of innocent helpless human life.

Opposition in the General Assembly was led by veteran Chittenden County Sen. John (Jack) O'Brien, and in late March the bill failed.

Feeling the weight of his years, and having reached the mandatory retirement age for bishops that had been set during Vatican II, Bishop Joyce stepped down late in 1971, taking up residence with other retired priests at St. Joseph's Home in Burlington. At first his health was poor, but he soon regained strength. Joyce received the title of apostolic administrator for three months until his successor took office. He kept up his exhausting correspondence. Indeed, one close associate said, "He never really retired." Many years later, in September 1985, the *Burlington Free Press* sent a reporter to visit. Maggie Maurice wrote:

> Bishop Robert F. Joyce lives in St. Joseph's home, a red brick building on the crest of South Prospect Street, and from his living room on the south side

Bishop Joyce and Baroness Maria Von Trapp at his retirement farewell — 1972.

you have a view of the city and the lake that ends with mountains looming like lavender curtains in the distant haze. It is a peaceful setting, surrounded by trees, and therefore an appropriate place to find Bishop Joyce. Now, at 88, he has been retired 13 years, but few men of his generation knew a more religious or stimulating life. He is a retired bishop of the Roman Catholic Church, but retired only in the sense that his official duties are over . . . On October 9, he'll be 89 years old. When he was 85, he said, "The best age is the age you are at."

In his room at St. Joseph's, Bishop Joyce sat with his feet up, reading the mail. "Doctors make me keep my feet up once in a while," he said. A nuisance, but he didn't mind. An afghan covered his long legs. His voice was strong, his smile warm. That hasn't changed. Last winter he was in the Fanny Allen Hospital for a month with bronchitis, flu, com-

Bp. John A. Marshall celebrating Bishop Joyce's funeral Mass at St. Michael's College Chapel.

plications, and stress. Stress? "I never learned not to work," he said . . . This summer he's almost back to his old schedule. He says mass in the chapel at the top of the stairs in the old part of St. Joseph's, calls on the sick and housebound, keeps up a voluminous correspondence . . .

When the old bishop's eyesight failed, Joyce turned to the telephone. Not long before his death, a nurse taking care of him would take the phone off the hook so that he could rest. After a brief nap, Joyce would begin wondering why nobody was calling him. So the phone was set back in its cradle, and it immediately began ringing.

During his retirement years, Joyce assembled his newspaper columns into a book. The last entry, titled "Golden Treasure," written on the last day of some year, read in part:

> The fleeting passage of the years, slipping by us like a rapid stream, gives us some faint conception of the transitory nature of life and of all created things. It should not be a cause of sadness but rather of joy, because it is fundamental in the Christian life that we have not here a lasting city, that we are on a pilgrimage, and that our goal is beyond the portals of time. If we are too attached to this world and this life, it may indicate that our concern for the real life, the life of grace here and the life of union in eternity, is weak and faltering . . . A good year passed is one that has been active mentally, morally, physically, according to one's abilities, in loving God and neighbor in the thousands of ways available. A good year to come is one that is offered, planned and dedicated to accomplish God's purpose and our own— that we may live.

In Bishop Joyce's final years, his successor John Marshall was a frequent visitor, the two men engaging in lengthy discussions of matters ranging from the church to the Boston Red Sox. Bishop Joyce died on September 1, 1990, nearing his 94th birthday.

Historian Tom Bassett said of him, nearly a decade later, "Ever since 1900 the Roman Catholic Church has been Vermont's largest denomination. It took a half century before Vermonters accepted that fact. It took Pat Joyce to make Vermonters say, 'We are not afraid of them anymore.'"

CHAPTER

8

IN THE AUTUMN OF 1978, Fr. John McSweeney was in Rome undertaking continuing education studies at the Vatican's North American College. Pope John Paul I had died in September and the College of Cardinals had convened, after a proper period of mourning, to choose a successor. McSweeney, an amateur historian, had gone to St. Peter's for the historic occasion of the Mass that opened the cardinals' gathering. He knew as he watched that soon one of the men present in the great church would be chosen the next pope. When the balloting began, Father McSweeney and fellow priests went to the Vatican each noon and evening to watch, and wait, among the assembled thousands, for the famous signal from the Sistine Chapel chimney, black smoke if no pope had been picked, white smoke if a choice had been made.

"We did this for three days," he recalled in 1999. "On the third evening, it was just getting dark, we saw the white smoke. The square was crowded, filled. I was standing with a priest who'd been through this before and he told me that within 10 or 15 minutes one of the cardinals would come out on the balcony and announce, '*Habemus papam,*' we have a Holy Father. We watched for the lights in the upper facade to come on, and soon they did.

Bp. John A. Marshall.

The big doors swung open and a cardinal stepped to the microphone and said, 'Habemus papam; Karol Wojtyla.' There was wild applause, though the Italians around me were saying, 'Que? Que? Que?' Who? Who? Who? But one of my fellow students, a Polish man, knew Cardinal Wojtyla personally. There were some Polish priests nearby and they were cheering, leaping around; they were absolutely elated."

Karol Wojtyla chose as the name for his pontificate that of his predecessor, John Paul, thus becoming Pope John Paul II. The new pope was to affect the political structure of the world and play a major role in bringing down the totalitarian regimes that had so long dominated and oppressed Eastern Europe, including his native Poland. The new Holy Father had, of course, less than two years before his elevation, walked the hills of Vermont. John Paul II's election would have its effect on the state. Indeed, the man who would serve as the seventh bishop of Burlington would become a friend of the new pope, and the pope would turn to him to undertake a major job for the Vatican. The new bishop of Burlington would be a man from Rome, though a New Englander by birth, a man schooled in, and to, the ways of Rome.

But to step back for a moment, upon the retirement of the popular Bishop Joyce, the Vatican had delivered unexpected orders with major repercussions for Vermont. Two New Englanders barely in their forties, one a Vermonter, were made bishops. It was late 1971 when Paul VI decreed that Joyce's right-hand man in Vermont, Msgr. Louis Gelineau, was to become a bishop. But the man who was known as "Rejoice" would not succeed his best friend at the helm of the Diocese of Burlington; he would go to Rhode Island and become head of one of the largest U.S. dioceses as bishop of Providence.

"I was thunderstruck," said Gelineau in 1998. "I was trembling, I was suddenly the youngest bishop in the entire country. But Bishop Joyce said, 'The church wants you to do it and you have to do it.'" The unease continued, Gelineau said, until the day he walked into Providence's cavernous Cathedral of St. Peter and St. Paul to become a bishop and to assume his new duties. The Vatican's apostolic delegate in Washington had wanted to preside. But Gelineau said no, it would be Bishop Joyce. And as Gelineau moved toward the altar with the great organ playing and the cathedral choir's voices soaring to the high rafters, his old friend and mentor was waiting by the altar. "It was then that I saw the other side," Gelineau said. "It was like the skies came down. My whole spirit was lifted up and I felt the world was mine. The people applauded and I sensed the true power of the church."

The Vatican works in unpredictable ways. For the vacant post in Vermont, it chose a Massachusetts man, a priest who had for some time been serving in Rome as business manager of the Vatican's North American College. Fr. John A. Marshall received word that he would be the seventh bishop of Burlington on the same day that Gelineau, in Burlington, got his marching orders for Rhode Island. A friend of Bishop Joyce's, Fr. Francis X. Gokey, S.S.E., happened to be in Rome at the time and wrote to Joyce:

> . . . Yesterday I met with Bishop-Elect Marshall. He had just come from a meeting with Cardinal Cicognani and was about to don for the first time the purple (borrowed from Bishop Hickey and a little tight around the waist) for a private audience with the Holy Father. He has a superb reputation here in Rome, especially at the North American College, as a very serious, hard-working and congenial person— one who never loses his "cool". His reputation was supported by my chat with him.

To Vermont was coming a man not even known to Bishop Joyce. It was just before Christmas and, in Burlington, assistant diocesan chancellor Father McSweeney was busy. Suddenly, to his seasonal responsibilities were added the tasks of preparing for the arrival and ordination of a new bishop. Bishop Marshall landed at Boston's Logan Airport on a sparkling winter day in mid-January. McSweeney was there to greet him with a delegation of Vermont churchmen. To make Marshall's arrival as trouble-free as possible,

Bishop Marshall's episcopal consecration – 1972.

Ruins of the cathedral – 1972.

Father McSweeney had used some Irish political connections to permit the new bishop to avoid going through airport customs. But when Marshall found out, he declined, and submitted to an inspection of his luggage, with agents rifling through vestments and gifts. "We found out that day that the bishop didn't cut corners," said McSweeney.

The episcopal ordination was held on January 25, 1972, in the Cathedral of the Immaculate Conception in Burlington. To a packed church, Bishop Marshall said, "Perhaps every newly appointed bishop would have the same thought, but because it is now only two months to the day since I received notification of my coming to you, one of my first impressions is still indelibly etched in my imagination: 'All those people! A whole state! Unbelievable! How does one manage?' The congregation of people gathered before me now and the representatives of every sector and interest of the diocese, who came to this Cathedral on Sunday, have only served to bring that same thought more vividly before me: bishop is for others."

(It is worth noting that two days after the ceremony, a committee in the Vermont Legislature endorsed the concept of abortion on demand during the first 12 weeks

Demolition of the cathedral.

of pregnancy. Vermont would soon find out how the new bishop stood on that matter.)

John Marshall grew up in Worcester, Massachusetts. According to Rev. Walter Miller, who worked with Marshall for many years, "Like a lot of Irish, they lived on the top floor of a three-decker house. Heat rose, and you could get a higher rent on the lower two floors." Ever studious and scholarly, but also a gifted athlete with a love of sports, John Marshall was the son of the Worcester postmaster. A valedictorian of his high school class, he graduated cum laude with a degree in English from Holy Cross College in Worcester and, for a time, enrolled in a seminary in Montreal. But the intensely bright student was soon off to Rome and the Vatican's training ground for bishops, the North American College. Ordained in 1953, he returned to his hometown as headmaster of a Catholic boys school. Then he went back to Rome for two tours of duty, ending up as "econome," or business manager, for the North American College. Working tirelessly, he gained praise for putting the college on firm financial ground. He was just finishing three years on the job when he was appointed to Vermont.

Just after his ordination, Marshall motored to Middlebury to preside, for his first time as bishop, at a confirmation. He had virtually no episcopal experience, and upon arrival, it showed. A local former seminarian, who greeted him, respectfully pointed out that the bishop's vestments were not properly donned. Some fast adjustments were made.

Back in Burlington, Marshall settled into the bishop's house at 52 South Williams Street. Used to spartan quarters in the Vatican, Marshall immediately felt uncomfortable in the large and ornate residence. He was just beginning to become acquainted with Vermont when a tragedy struck, on March 14, 1972. Father McSweeney remembered, "I was living at St. Anthony's (in Burlington's South End) and Fr. Rosario Morency woke me. He said the cathedral was on fire. I'll never forget the scene. The building was totally engulfed. We stood in front of the place. There was a sense of helplessness. Nothing could be saved, it went up so fast. Father Morency said, 'There is nothing we can do. Let's go home.' We did."

So the great stone edifice that was Bishop de Goesbriand's pride, Burlington's Cathedral of the Immaculate Conception, 105 years old, was gone, damaged beyond repair. The chapel was saved, as well as the precious diocesan records, some dating to 1830. The records would form the heart of what would become the diocesan archive. Taken from the chapel, with only the slightest damage, was the ornate Altar of St. Peter in Chains, which held the single link from the Roman chain believed to have bound St. Peter, the precious artifact de Goesbriand had long ago brought from Rome. The high stone walls of the building remained and, miraculously, the gilded statue of Our Lady of Lourdes, the gift of Bishop Michaud, still gleamed atop the highest tower. But the wrecker's ball would soon fall on the gutted building, and the statue would find a new home, at the Shrine of St. Anne on Isle La Motte. A former altar boy who confessed to setting the fire was sent to a mental institution. Long, often difficult negotiations and endless planning sessions followed. For a time thought was given to designating St. Joseph's Church as the cathedral. But eventually, a new, modernistic, and much smaller Cathedral of the Immaculate Conception was to be built, on the site of the old cathedral.

Aside from dealing with the cathedral's destruction, Marshall found himself administering a diocese still coming to terms with the revolutionary dictates of Vatican II. New orders kept arriving from Rome. McSweeney recalled, "The rituals were in three-ring binders, and they were changing all the time. It was a job trying to keep up." Bishop Marshall completed the process of adapting the Catholic Church in Vermont to the changes brought about by Vatican II.

The bishop hired, as his second secretary, a Burlington woman, Mary McClintock. She would serve him throughout his nearly 20 year term. She said in 1999, "He worked 18 hour days, seven days a week. The only time he took off was a two-week vacation on Cape Cod, in August. Then for a week in February he went to the Carthusian Monastery on Mount Equinox. He had a tiny room there and slept on straw. Heat was a little woodstove

Carthusian Monastery, Manchester, built 1967–72.

that he kept going himself. He had a chair, table, lamp, and kneeler. He said that when he walked down the hallway that connected the rooms there was ice on the walls. He would pray and reflect. He enjoyed it."

McClintock continued, "Every day he was in Burlington, he was up and out for his morning walk at six-thirty. He walked about a mile up North Avenue and back, no matter what the weather, for as long as it took him to say the Rosary. In the early years, he also did the air force exercise routine out on the back porch, and sometimes he shot hoops in the gym. He said Mass every day in the orphanage chapel, and every day he said a brief homily, off the top of his head. But his speeches were always written, very carefully organized. If he was traveling and got back late, he would go and say Mass late at night. He never missed it. And he *had* to go to confession regularly. I never could understand it. Here was this man who led a Christ-like life and yet, he had to go to confession."

According to McSweeney, "He never directed a conversation to himself. He was not in the least self-centered. It was hard to get things out of him. He took meticulous notes, in beautiful handwriting. He wrote constantly. He wrote far into the night on profound, academic subjects. Unlike Joyce, he never gave the same talk twice. And those talks were so deep they would go over the heads of people. You almost needed a knowledge of theology. He never mixed in a story, a joke. With Marshall, you had better know what you were talking about. He was wonderful to work with, wonderful. He was a churchman. And he was a teacher."

McClintock said that Marshall worked in his private quarters into the night, then around nine o'clock would phone some old friends in Massachusetts, often to talk sports. Marshall was a diehard supporter of the Boston Red Sox and Boston Celtics. He also made, in McClintock's words, a "yearly pilgrimage" to South Bend, Indiana, with some close friends from his Worcester days, to attend a Notre Dame football game. Father Miller said, "He lived very simply. His only joy was sports. He was almost addicted. I was in the hospital for a month and he would come and see me. He would get into these discussions with one of the floor nurses for a solid half hour on baseball. I hated baseball. Once he overstayed in White River Junction watching the World Series. He was behind schedule and he got picked up for speeding in Randolph. He paid the ticket." Miller also said, "He was a great mimic. Once I saw him do a perfect imitation of Cardinal Spellman."

In time, Marshall sold the grand brick residence on Burlington's South Williams Street to the Vermont Medical Center, and it was demolished to make way for a parking lot. (Much of the woodwork and some furnishings can still be seen, in a building on Winooski's West Canal Street that in 1999 housed an Oriental restaurant, and in the University of Vermont's Grasse Mount building.) Marshall moved into two rooms in the remodeled diocesan office building on Burlington's North Avenue, which better suited his preferred living style. "He said he didn't know how to live in a house," McClintock recalled. Bishop Joyce had loved the big and rather ornate South Williams Street house, but people were coming to realize that in Marshall, Vermont had just about the opposite of Bishop Joyce.

Bishop Gelineau became acquainted with Marshall and said, in 1998, "He was hard to get to know. He was an intellectual, a theological scholar. He had the Rome mentality: the church comes first. He wasn't the lovable, fatherly type Joyce was." McClintock recalled, "Bishop Marshall didn't like social functions. He was shy; he found it hard to talk to people, unless you were talking about the church. Then he would talk on and on." Father McSweeney said, "He was uncomfortable in social situations, hated cocktail parties. He didn't drink, except for a glass of wine."

The scholarly cleric had arrived in Vermont at a time of change and considerable turmoil. The Vietnam War was raging, though the negotiations had begun that would eventually end it. Vietnamese children, war refugees, were among the children being housed at the diocesan child center. One little boy slept each night on the stairs, some war time terror making it impossible for him to sleep in a bed. Demonstrators were in the streets demanding peace and U.S. disengagement. Politically, once rock-ribbed conservative and Republican Vermont was becoming increasingly Democratic and liberal. In 1964, Vermont had elected its first Democratic governor since the Civil War. In 1972, the state put in office its first Catholic chief executive, Thomas Salmon, of Bellows Falls. Then, in 1974, upon the retirement of longtime Republican U.S. Sen. George D. Aiken, Catholic former county prosecutor Patrick J. Leahy was elected to the Senate, another first for Vermont Catholics. The Vermont Legislature, in 1973, approved public welfare funding for abortion. Bishop Marshall made known his opposition, in no uncertain terms. A considerable number of Catholic state legislators came to seek his advice on the difficult issue and found him intransigent. The church's doctrine he held to be unshakable. And in 1973 came the U.S. Supreme Court's landmark *Roe vs. Wade* ruling, which legalized abortion. Marshall quickly made known his unequivocal opposition. Throughout his Vermont episcopacy, he attended anti-abortion rallies, not usually up front delivering speeches but somewhere in the crowd, quiet and often unrecognized.

When Republican Richard A. Snelling was elected governor, taking office in 1976, he asked Sister Elizabeth Candon, R.S.M., the popular president of Trinity College, to become head of the Vermont Department of Social Welfare. Candon, a lifelong Democrat, accepted, and soon was at odds with the bishop, particularly when she announced her support for public funding of abortion. Secretary Candon and the bishop met in private, though nobody but the two ever knew just what was said. She stayed on the job. To Burlington and the bishop's residence came Governor Snelling, an administrator often known for his use of personal intimidation, for a meeting with Bishop Marshall, apparently convinced that the bishop was interfering with state government. An observer recalled that the two men had not even gotten into the bishop's office before the shouting started. "Nobody was ever going to tell Bishop Marshall how to run the diocese," Mary McClintock said, and the governor, of course, was not about to take orders from the bishop.

When the Equal Rights Amendment came up for a ratification vote in the Legislature, Marshall announced his opposition. "There is a possibility that the ERA referendum . . . will further endanger the right to life of the unborn," Marshall said in a letter sent to all parishes. "Accordingly, although the intended purpose of the ERA legislation fully deserves our support, that end cannot justify the possibility of further endangering the life of every unborn being, male and female." Women's groups were furious. The ERA failed in the Vermont General Assembly. "It was the only legislative issue Bishop Marshall ever won in Vermont," according to Father McSweeney. The victory further solidified Marshall's reputation as an arch conservative. In contrast, Marshall was a strong advocate of ecumenical efforts, and served as president of the Vermont Ecumenical Council. He was also deeply concerned about the Vietnam War, saying in an interview that he believed it to be a product of American materialism. (But he later said that Catholics should be prepared to die for their country.) Then, in 1982, Bishop Marshall joined a minority of American bishops in expressing deep opposition to a pastoral letter opposing any further nuclear weapons testing and production.

Despite the controversy, Bishop Marshall remained in favor with Rome. As his secretary noted, "He was very much by the book. This is what the church teaches. This is *it*." Father Miller said, "He was a micromanager, of the whole diocese." Marshall returned to Rome on a regular basis and had become acquainted with John Paul II. McClintock said, "He knew the pope. But he always said he was amazed that the pope knew him."

In 1981, the Vatican summoned the bishop to Rome, where the Holy Father appointed him to head a detailed study of American seminaries. It would be a formidable job, and Marshall assured the priests of his diocese that the additional work would not impact the diocese. Bishop Gelineau recalled, "The pope saw the need to look at the training of priests in this country. Bishop Marshall organized 10 teams of bishops, theologians, and teachers to visit all the seminaries in the United States. They visited all the high-school-level, postgraduate, and college seminaries, more than 150 of them. It was a massive job. The seminaries were worried; it looked like a hatchet job. But he did a masterful job. He sent thousands of pages of reports to Rome. Much seminary training was not preparing priests to deal well with the world. Bishop Marshall changed that. The study was tremendously valuable."

At the same time, Marshall kept up with his duties as bishop. He addressed the growing need for new facilities for Fanny Allen Hospital. The little hospital was still operating in the old hotel long ago purchased from Michael Kelly. The hospital had become particularly beloved of country people, who preferred to have their ailments treated in the small, homey facility, rather than in one of the nearby Burlington hospitals. Marshall set in motion plans for building a new Fanny Allen Hospital in Colchester, next to the old hotel, which was eventually dismantled.

Meanwhile, Mary McClintock worked closely with Marshall on the seminary study. She said, "For each seminary there was a report at least an

Sr. Annunciata and C. Douglas Cairns – 1966.

inch thick. It was very detailed. It was highly confidential. The reports went to Rome and the seminaries got a report back from Rome." The study lasted more than eight years, and Marshall met each year with the pope to discuss the study's progress. McClintock said, "They had lunch and dinner. He was amazed how aware the pope was of what was going on with the study. Also, he would say that the pope didn't understand the impact of the American media on the church over here. He talked to him about it, and he saw that the pope came to appreciate that impact." John McSweeney, the only monsignor Marshall appointed in his nearly two decades in Vermont, remembered, "He

Administrative board – 1984.

seemed to think and act like the pope. He was in Rome so much on the seminary study. Things he would write you'd see in the Holy Father's writings."

The study concluded in 1989. There had been reports during the time that Rome had bigger things in store for Bishop Marshall. Rumor had him becoming archbishop of some large city, perhaps Baltimore, even Chicago. During his time in Vermont, according to McClintock, Bishop Marshall had recorded, on tape, the happenings of his everyday life. The tapes were transcribed by Marie Collins, who had once served Bishops Ryan and Joyce, and were distributed each month to Vermont priests serving outside the diocese. Marshall's December 1991 tape included the following passage, describing the day the Vatican once more brought sudden change to the Burlington diocese:

> On Monday, December 16 . . . the rest of the afternoon was spent with Fr. McSweeney and Fr. Jay Haskin, and I was already on my way upstairs, when Mrs. Polly Real, a secretary at the diocese caught me and said there was a telephone call from the Pro-Nuncio. Would I take it? I went back to the office and was told that the Holy Father had nominated me to succeed Bishop Maguire as Bishop of Springfield, Mass. After so many rumors, it was a relief in that sense to have "the shoe drop." The other side of the coin is that I have said and still believe that "there's no place like Vermont." We have our problems like everyone else

but they are somewhat manageable and the Bishop has direct knowledge of what is going on rather than learning everything through third parties. Archbishop Cacciavillan spoke of the appointment as an honor; Springfield is twice as large in numbers of people and a quarter the size in area. He was encouraging me to accept but, as far as I was concerned, that was never a question. If the Holy Father asks anyone to do something, I know enough about the operation to realize that there has been a great deal of discussion; other names have been eliminated for some reason or another; and the designee is expected to accept.

So Bishop Marshall went back to his native Massachusetts. Father McSweeney said, "He loved Burlington. He had found his niche. He really hated to leave Vermont." Marshall took up residence in the huge old house that was the bishop of Springfield's home. But the man who by his own admission had never learned to live in a house never unpacked, until Mary McClintock and her husband went to Springfield and helped him take things out of boxes.

Just before leaving Vermont, Marshall had recommended to Rome that Father McSweeney be appointed a monsignor. That appointment came through after Marshall departed; the Burlington priest was also named interim administrator of the diocese.

Strange, sometimes, seem the ways of the Vatican. To Vermont to serve as the eighth bishop of Vermont came a Rhode Island man, the longtime auxiliary bishop of Providence. Kenneth Angell had for nearly two decades served as second in command to Vermonter Louis Gelineau, bishop of Providence, and the two had become close friends. Meanwhile, as Easter Sunday, 1992, approached, Marshall sent a note to the McClintocks:

> Dear Mary and Rit,
> Just this morning I figured out why I missed Vermont so much but have not been devastated by the move. It's the Mystical Body of Christ!
> My answer had been that I'm doing the same work of a priest that I've always done, so what difference does location make? The proper answer is that I'm still working together with every person with whom I've ever been associated in the Church (indeed, everyone in the Church everywhere) because of our union in Christ, the Eucharist, the other sacraments, in faith itself.

No reason why I should not have figured that out before. I preferred not to try and even today the thought just came as a "distraction" in meditation.

My prayers and best wishes for a most joyful Easter season for all the family.

Devotedly yours in Christ
+ J. A. M.

Marshall served as bishop of Springfield for only two and a half years. In February 1994, he phoned Mary McClintock to tell her he was undergoing medical tests. Marshall, who but for back pains had always been healthy while in Vermont, was soon diagnosed with inoperable bone cancer. The disease was relentless; eventually Bishop Marshall was confined to bed. The archbishop of Boston, Bernard Cardinal Law, visited him on June 7, 1994, and wrote to Bishop Angell, in Burlington, the next day:

> Your excellency,
>
> . . . As I write to you, my prayer is that the good Lord will take Bishop John Marshall to Himself very soon. He is prepared for death as few persons I have ever known. My visits with him have been mini retreats. Thank you and all those in the Diocese of Burlington for supporting him with your prayers and with your love during this critical time.

John Marshall died on July 3, 1994. The funeral was held on a hot summer day in Springfield, and many Vermonters attended. A memorial service followed at the cathedral in Burlington. "Burlington was on his mind when he was dying," Mary McClintock said. "Right near the end, at his bedside, he gave a talk to a group of young priests, for almost an hour. He steeled himself for that. He was always a teacher. There were people who said he might be a saint. I think we had an extraordinary opportunity to know such a man. He lived his life every minute the way Christ expects us to do."

CHAPTER

9
_____

HISTORY HAPPENED on October
5, 1999, in Burlington's Old North
End. And well it might have on a
day when Lake Champlain mir-
rored a sky filled with heavy, un-
broken clouds, the kind of a
day when Vermonters are in-
clined to look back rather than
contemplate the onset of the
winter everywhere foretold.
Even the colored leaves of the
maples were dulled that
steelgray day. To Vermont's
largest church came more than
1,000 of the Catholic faithful,
among them Bernard Cardinal
Law, archbishop of Boston, the
Most Reverend Gabriel Montalvo,
the Vatican's apostolic nuncio to the
United States, and 38 bishops from
throughout the nation. All had gathered to
celebrate a special Mass marking the 25th an-
niversary of episcopal ordination of the eighth bishop of Burlington, Kenneth Anthony Angell.

Bp. Kenneth Angell.

It was an occasion of splendid music and great ceremony. A wonderful
choir, the brasses of the Vermont Symphony Orchestra, and thunderous organ music sounded forth from the balcony of St. Joseph's Church. The monks
of the Weston Priory sang. Words of praise and affection were spoken for
Bishop Angell. Cardinal Law said, "You have truly lived your motto, serving
the Lord with gladness." Angell's old friend, Bp. Louis Gelineau, speaking in

the church where, he noted, his parents had been married exactly 77 years ago that day, said "What unites us all is the regard and love we have for Bishop Angell . . . You have indeed served the Lord with gladness." Having heard an eloquent homily from Gelineau, and many other words of praise, Bishop Angell rose to deliver his response. Calling on his well-known reserve of humor, he began by saying, "Bishop Gelineau, I would like to know who you were talking about. I'd like to meet him some time." Then Bishop Angell's voice became serious and he said, "Once you start to follow Jesus, there is no turning back. He has been with me constantly."

While the pageantry of the grand occasion will be long remembered, it is likely that an announcement uttered near the start of the ceremonies will emerge as the grand day's truly historic moment. Monsignor McSweeney, a Burlington native, stepped to the microphone to read a message sent by the Vatican. The monsignor delivered the news that the great church of St. Joseph, the pride of Burlington's French Catholics for nearly a century and a half, had been recognized by the Holy Father as the co-cathedral of the Diocese of Burlington. The news came as a joyous surprise for the members of the old parish, and was greeted with sustained applause. What is certainly the largest, and perhaps the grandest, of all Vermont's churches had, it seemed, finally received long-overdue recognition.

But it is not always within such majestic settings that the eighth bishop of Burlington performs his duties. The chill in the fall air that memorable October day recalled a cold and starry night three days before Christmas in 1998, with an icy wind cutting in from Lake Champlain, as Bishop Angell arrived at the grim Corrections Center in St. Albans to celebrate Mass. Having been cleared through metal detectors after handing his change and watch to an attendant, the bishop donned his robes and miter in a small anteroom. In the spotless, tile-floored prison gymnasium, a 20 voice choir and some 60 inmates awaited his arrival. With the entry of the bishop, the choir raised its voice in song:

> Sing choir of angels,
> Sing in exultation.
> Oh come ye, oh come ye,
> To Bethlehem.

The music echoed and reechoed off the cinder-block walls, making the score of voices sound, as the bishop later observed, "like the Mormon Tabernacle Choir, or perhaps I should say the Vatican Choir." The bishop entered impressively; all eyes turned to the large bespectacled man walking with his crosier into the basketball court temporarily made a house of worship. As the service began, the bishop said, "We acknowledge that we are sinners, all of us, and we ask the Lord to be merciful." And he said, "I know it is difficult for you. You are away from home. You are in a strange place. You're as anxious as Mary and Joseph were fleeing with the Christ Child from Herod into a strange land. But you are blessed in one sense. You have time, time to meditate on the true meaning of Christmas. If you had been the only person born into this world Christ would have suffered and died for you, and you, and you."

The Mass was said, more hymns were sung, and a deacon spoke to thank the bishop for having come to the prison, once again, at Christmastime. Then the deacon said to his captive audience, "We hope to see you all next year." The bishop immediately raised his hand. "There's one thing," he interjected, "I'd like to correct you on. I hope I don't see all of you here next year." The remark was greeted with instant applause.

With the service ended, cookies and soda were served and everyone milled about, talking, even laughing. The bishop moved among the inmates in friendly conversation. A man in his mid-forties, with graying beard, told Bishop Angell they had met in a place known as "the Castle" in Cranston, Rhode Island, 23 years before. The Castle, the man explained, is inmate slang for the Rhode Island State Penitentiary. "You were there at Christmas, with Bishop Gelineau," the prisoner said. The two men talked quietly, then the inmate confided of Bishop Angell, "He used to come there all the time, to visit us."

On the drive back to Burlington, Bishop Angell talked of his visits to prisons. The first had, indeed, occurred in Rhode Island.

> Every year, Bishop Gelineau was invited to go to the prisons by their chaplain. When I became a bishop, they invited me. The first time I went they were showing a movie, I'll never forget the name of it, *A Rage to Kill*. The prisoners had a choice between the movie and the Mass and only two of them came to Mass. One of them was this man who asked me to remember his father in my Mass. He told me that his father had died of a broken heart. Then he said, "I broke his heart." He cried through the whole Mass. It touched me. Christ established this priesthood so that we reach out to the poorest of the poor, not only to the materialistically poor, but to the spiritually poor. That is how it all began. The people in the prisons, they are a group of people who need Christ. They can't come out. Particularly at Christmastime, it is better that we go to them.

Kenneth Angell is a Rhode Islander. "When I was made the bishop of Burlington I was 62 and I was seated at a desk, in Providence, about a mile from where I was born," he recalled one day in his Burlington office. Angell grew up poor in and around Providence. "I was raised in a loving family," he recalled. "Neither of my parents had graduated from high school. They married in 1928 and I was born in 1930. I have a brother and a sister. It was the depression. My father lost his job. They had to give up their apartment. We all moved into my grandmother's house. My mother got a job first. Finally my father found work, and we got an apartment again. We had a happy childhood. There were no luxuries in life. We went from apartment to apartment. We couldn't afford a house."

Though Catholic from birth, Angell attended public schools because "the Catholic school was too far to walk." He says that as a child he was discriminated against because he was "a public school kid." He recalled, "At Mass, those of us who did not attend a Catholic school were made to sit on the side, and we were not allowed to say the prayers. I felt like a second-class citizen. It was a good lesson in life, to be careful of that kind of thing."

Angell was in fourth grade when he began to think about becoming a priest. He told his parents, and they were supportive. He entered Our Lady of Providence Seminary at the end of the ninth grade and spent five years there. "Three of us who were together at the seminary became bishops," he said. "I made wonderful friends; some are still my friends. The priesthood can be a very lonely life. It can be a beautiful life, but you do need friends."

From the Rhode Island seminary, Angell went to St. Mary's Seminary in Baltimore. "My parents said to me once, when they were driving me down there, 'If you want to come home, home is always there. We will understand.' They were wonderful, always supportive." Angell recalled his years in Baltimore as "very happy." "The Sulpicians taught us well," he said. Angell had thus been trained by the same religious order that had instructed the young Louis de Goesbriand. He returned to Baltimore for a year of work as a proctor at his old school, Our Lady of Providence. Then he was ordained at the great Cathedral of St. Peter and St. Paul in Providence on May 26, 1956. First sent to a parish on Jamestown Island in Narragansett Bay, young Father Angell was bitten by a dog on his way to hear his first confessions. Otherwise, his summer on the island was enjoyable. He went on to serve in a parish in Providence for four years, and in a Newport parish for eight years. As a parish priest Angell baptized his 84 year-old grandfather, a retired ship's captain. He recalled, "My grandmother had prayed for that every day, for him to be baptized. He had a stroke just a week or two later. He was never again conscious."

Being a parish priest in Newport "was fascinating," Angell said. "In the parish were the poorest of the poor and the richest of the rich. John Kennedy,

Bishop Angell's installation.

when he was president, used to come to our church. He would be staying at his wife's childhood home, Hammersmith Farm, and he brought his family to Mass. He always said hello. And he would tell the priest how much he had enjoyed the sermon. I got to know the servants in those great Newport houses. In one, the help would have a whist party in the great hall, for the benefit of the church, when the owners were away. Those were wonderful years. I always hoped I could go back as a pastor to Newport. It didn't happen."

It didn't happen because, in 1968, Angell was invited to the cathedral in Providence to become secretary to Russell McVinney, bishop of Providence. Angell accepted. McVinney died in 1971. His successor was a Vermonter, the new bishop of Providence, Louis Gelineau. Angell quickly learned that Gelineau "really didn't know anything about Rhode Island." He had to learn fast. So on a chilly day just after Christmas, 1971, Father Angell arrived in Burlington to deliver to Gelineau a briefcase full of information about the Catholic Church in the Ocean State. Stepping from his automobile at the Bishop Joyce/Gelineau residence on South Williams Street, Angell slipped on a patch of ice, and broke a leg in several places. It was his first time in Vermont. "I was the one," he said, "who was supposed to be taking the new bishop around Rhode Island and I was on crutches." Despite the slippery start to their association, Angell and Gelineau became a highly effective team. "Bishop Gelineau is like a brother to me," said Angell in 1999. "In 21 years, we've never had a harsh word."

On August 13, 1974, Angell was appointed auxiliary bishop of Providence. When the word came from Rome, Angell was "dumbfounded." He recalled, "The only thing I had ever known for sure was that I wouldn't be a bishop one day. I only have two bachelor degrees. I had really only wanted to go back to my parish in Newport. I tried to protest it." The night he learned of his appointment, Father Angell paced the floor until the wee hours. He sought the advice of Bishop Gelineau, who said, "You can call the delegate, but it won't do any good." Angell recalled, "In those days, you were given a coded message of acceptance to send to the apostolic nuncio in Washington. Mine was, 'The October Report Will Be Forthcoming.' I went to the telegraph office and found it jammed with people. Everyone was sending telegrams to Washington to impeach Nixon. My telegram was delayed. The nuncio's office called. 'Yes,' I said, 'I've sent the message.' "

Angell was ordained bishop on October 7, 1974, in Providence's Cathedral of St. Peter and St. Paul, designed by Patrick Keeley, who had also drafted plans for the old cathedral in Burlington. Angell was very uneasy as he entered the building. "I had this unrest," he said. "I even thought of going out a side door. But at the imposition of hands, at the conferral, and I must say I have never had any visions in my life, I suddenly felt this tremendous peace. I thought, 'Once you start to serve Christ, there is no turning back.' I thought of those words."

Angell served for 18 years as Providence's auxiliary bishop. "It was kind of like being lieutenant governor," he said. "I did many ceremonial things. I was on all kinds of committees. Bishop Gelineau and I worked together beautifully." There was one frustration, Angell noted, with being second in command. "Unless you're the lead dog," he said, "the view never changes." In the fall of 1992, he moved to the front as word came that he had been appointed bishop of Burlington. "I was summoned to Vermont," he said. "It was difficult to move, to pull up roots and go, I must admit. I was 62, I'd

Left to Right: Msgr. John McSweeney, Bishop Angell, Bishop Gelineau, Msgr. John Fradet (standing), Msgr. Edwin Buckley.

been in Rhode Island all my life. Most of my friends were there. When I broke my leg, in Burlington, I vowed I'd never go back to the place. But the Lord, it seems, has a sense of humor."

Angell was installed in ceremonies on November 9, 1992, in St. Michael the Archangel Chapel on the campus of St. Michael's College in Colchester.

On a January day in 1999, more than six years after becoming bishop of Burlington, Kenneth Angell talked about his Vermont years. From his office on Burlington's North Avenue, the west-facing window of which commands one of Vermont's finest views, a pale sun could be seen low over the Adirondack Mountains, casting a strange bluish light on the chill waters of Lake Champlain. He said, "I have been happy here. The people of Vermont are just the opposite of what I thought they would be. I thought they would be cold and distant. But I have found them warm and receptive. The priests of this diocese are a fine group of people. Most of them are in rural parishes, at a considerable distance from one another. When they gather together, it's like a kind of celebration. They're so busy. They have little help. There is no time for pettiness. I've particularly enjoyed my pastoral visits. So many people here say they have never talked to a bishop before. I visit a parish for a weekend. I meet with the parish councils, say Mass, preach a sermon. I get to know the people. It has been wonderful."

A month earlier, a few days after Christmas, Bishop Angell, as he does each year, had attended the annual luncheon held for seminarians at the University of Vermont's Newman Center. The guests of honor were several young men, mostly Vermonters, studying for the priesthood. Some 30 Vermont priests were in attendance. The bishop spoke in the chapel, directing his remarks at the aspiring priests:

> I know this can be a difficult time as you prepare for the priesthood. Is God really calling me to be a priest? We worry about our families. We worry about what we might be able to do with a family of our own. We have to trust in the Lord. From Christ Jesus we get our strength to overcome these difficulties we have. I recall a story, the story of a man who was standing on the top of a cliff, taking a photograph. Suddenly, the ground gave way and he was falling. But he reached out and grabbed a bush. Hanging there, he asked the Lord for help. A voice replied, "Let go of the bush." The man said, "Is there anyone else up there?" It takes faith. God has loved us and we can't explain why. Christ came into this world to bring us to heaven. But do we really, really appreciate it? . . . This is one of the

blessings I have received in coming to Vermont. We have a group of wonderful priests. You seminarians, you are our hope. Thank you for all the sacrifices you are making. Thank you, all, for doing the work of Christmas all year long.

After the service, Justin Baker, a native of Essex Junction and a 1988 graduate of UVM, talked about his decision to become a priest. Baker said, "You know, my parish priest never asked me if I might be interested in the priesthood. Our bishop has no fear of asking any young man, who's not married, if he's thought of becoming a priest. We have to do that."

Bishop Angell recalled that day with the seminarians, as he discussed the challenges facing his church in Vermont. The man destined to shepherd the Catholic Church in Vermont into the new millennium talked about the troublesome problem of finding enough priests to serve the Diocese of Burlington:

> When I came here we had four young men studying for the priesthood. That was nowhere near enough to meet our needs. I did a lot of thinking and praying about how to attract young men to the priesthood. Now we have established this "House of Discernment" at the Newman Center at UVM. People can go there and spend a night, two weeks,

Bishop Angell at the House of Discernment.

a month, whatever. They can discuss spiritual matters, the possibilities of becoming priests. We have two priests there to help them. Many come and decide they are not being called. But we now have 12 men in various stages of preparing for the priesthood. It's very encouraging.

He continued, "We've tried to involve women in the diocese. We have a women's commission for the diocese, to give women a greater voice. Our development director is a woman, as is our director of Catholic Charities. Our superintendent and assistant superintendent of schools are women. A woman is the chair of our board of education. If a priest is not required, I've tried to give the job to a woman. We've appointed two women to the Diocesan Board of Administration, a nun and a lay woman."

The bishop said that he has worked to modernize the diocese. A diocesan priorities conference has been established to study the need for new programs, to determine whether some old programs may have run their course. A real estate committee is in place.

The bishop talked of the future:

> We need to expand our House of Discernment. We need to encourage more young men to become priests. So many of our priests are getting older. We need to network the diocese by computer. We need a retreat center for the diocese, for our priests. I dream about that. We need to help people with AIDS. Many of them are the poorest of the poor. Many have been rejected, even by their families. Many can't work. I would like to increase benefits for our retired priests. We need to reach out more to people newly arriving in our state, to the Vietnamese, for instance.

Bishop Angell is a man who enjoys people. His large black car is much on the roads as he travels the state to meet the people. Fr. Walter Miller, diocesan chancellor, is usually at the wheel. "Affable, gregarious, holy," are words Miller uses to describe Angell. "He likes to get together with fellow priests. He always has a book going. He knows show tunes, old movies." Angell himself says he is an avid reader of books, particularly of Dickens. He loves to gather with fellow priests, and used to do it often on Cape Cod. While he has made many friends in Vermont, he still has a large cadre of acquaintances back in Rhode Island. In planning the celebration of the 25th anniversary of his consecration as bishop, Angell saw to it that festivities would be held not only at St. Joseph's in Burlington, but also in Providence.

*A banquet in the Hotel Vermont dining room, Burlington,
for laity and representatives of various religious orders.*

Angell is deeply concerned, in his words, about "respect life issues." His official biography states that "his key concern definitely centers around respect life issues, from the unborn to the elderly. He is a leading spokesperson for the church on such matters as abortion, assisted suicide, euthanasia, capital punishment, medical and genetic ethics and care for the elderly. He is quite visible not only in Catholic respect life activities, but in ecumenical right-to-life efforts as well." Angell is also concerned about problems of violence worldwide, and often uses speaking opportunities, such as graduations and banquets, to discuss such subjects. He became personally involved in the campaign, which began in 1995, to bring about a worldwide ban on land mines. He keeps a close watch on the Vermont Legislature, ready to fight any attempt to resurrect the death penalty. Angell is also involved in matters ecumenical and is vice president of the Vermont Ecumenical Council and Bible Society. While Bishop Marshall often quietly attended pro-life events, sometimes unnoticed in the crowd, Bishop Angell is often seen in the front row or leading a procession. Angell is well aware that not all of his positions are widely popular. But he says of his church, "It is what it is. It has changed, over the years. But it is what it is."

Of particular interest to Bishop Angell are Vermont's religious orders. "I recall," said the bishop, "that Pope Pius XII once said that the glory of the church in the United States are the parochial schools and the religious who teach in the schools. The value of the religious orders in Vermont has been incalculable. The good they have done is almost immeasurable."

Let us digress for a bit to take note of some of the orders that today make Vermont their home. To Burlington in 1872, at the request of Bishop de Goesbriand, came the Sisters of Mercy, to be teachers in the Catholic schools of Vermont. Sister Jeannine Mercure, president of the Burlington order, recalled in 1999 that when she joined the order in 1963, there were nearly 200 members in Burlington alone. "The Sisters of Mercy staffed Cathedral High School. Forty of them taught at that school," she said, seated in the quiet of an October afternoon at Mount St. Mary's Convent in Burlington, the imposing, turreted, Victorian structure on Burlington's ridge-top Mansfield Avenue.

But times have changed, and as the number of Catholic schools declined in Vermont, the sisters took on other tasks, teaching at Trinity College and at a handful of Catholic schools. They also operate a hospitality wing in Burlington for women who have hospitalized relatives. They run a retreat house in the town of Benson called Lumen Christi. The sisters operate a prison ministry and visit the sick. They are planning to open an affordable housing complex in Burlington in the near future. One sister works with undocumented aliens along the Mexican border in New Mexico. Another serves on an Indian reservation in North Dakota. In 1999, there were just 80 Sisters of Mercy in Burlington. Still, "There is plenty of work for us to do," said Sister Jeannine.

Sister M. Joan Caron recalled the day 72 years ago when she arrived, from her Grand Isle County home, as a teenager at Mount St. Mary's, to begin a religious life. "I had no doubt in my mind that God was calling me, calling me to be a Sister of Mercy. The parish priest drove my mother and me here. It was freezing cold. We prayed the car would get through to Burlington. My father was a doctor and he was delivering a baby that day. He couldn't come. My mother was a little teary. The first night was scary. I was lonesome. The floors creaked. There were slivers in the floor. It reminded me of a barn." Sister Joan is proud of her long years of teaching. "I taught French, Latin, Greek, physics, mathematics, religion, history, everything but English. I have had a truly wonderful life."

On the hilltop overlooking Lake Memphremagog, at Newport, a convent stands beside the church called St. Mary Star of the Sea, the edifice built by the persistent Father Clermont. That grand church was, for more than six decades, filled with music directed by Sister Edmund of Jesus. Sister Edmund, who died in 1999, was a member of the Daughters of Charity of the Sacred Heart of Jesus, whose Newport mission was founded in 1905 with the arrival of four nuns from France. The Daughters of Charity have ever since been teachers in the Catholic schools of Newport. "There were 61 sisters here when I came in 1931," Sister Edmund said shortly before her death. "Now there are only eight. Two of us are still working in the schools. At Sacred Heart High School, all the teachers were sisters, except the coach. I taught music. I still do. I began as choir director in 1938, with the younger choir. I have choir members who have been with me for 50 years."

Sister Edmund was born Marthe Savard in Chicoutimi, Quebec. She began to learn music at age seven, with piano lessons. "I never wanted to enter a religious order," she recalled, "but I heard this call. The call was very strong. Just before my first vows I went to the provincial. I said, 'I don't know. I am wondering if I can keep this all my life.' She said, 'You know, the door is open. You can go home.' I said that I was afraid I would not have the courage to do this all my life. She said it was a temptation, that I wouldn't feel it after my vows. She was right."

The young nun took her father's name when she took her vows at the age of 15 and became, thereafter, Sister Edmund of Jesus. She studied the violin in Montreal, and majored in music at college. Then she studied in Paris with the legendary teacher of music Nadia Boulanger. A priest once said of Sister Edmund's choir at St. Mary Star of the Sea, "Your choir prays with music."

At one time, Sister Edmund directed a band, an orchestra, and five choirs. In 1973, she conducted the Vermont All-state Music Festival. She has received a certificate from the Friends of the Vermont Symphony Orchestra and was awarded the Benemerenti Medal for long and inspired service to her church. On the wall of her office, by her piano, is a plaque presented to her in 1988 by former pupils:

We Gratefully Acknowledge
55 years
Of Dedicated Service by
SISTER EDMUND OF JESUS
In the Promotion of Music.
The sound of music from the top of Sacred
Heart Hill and across Lake Memphremagog
Will always echo in our hearts.

Sister Edmund of Jesus died in Newport on December 12, 1999.
In Colchester, in a convent adjacent to the Fanny Allen Hospital, live the

remaining Vermont members of the Religious Hospitalers of St. Joseph. The first American member of the order, founded at Montreal in 1644, was Fanny Allen, daughter of Ethan Allen. The sisters were nurses, and once they staffed the Fanny Allen and De Goesbriand Hospitals and Burlington's St. Joseph's Home for the Aged. But in the fall of 1999 there were but 17 members of the order at Colchester, and six of them were living in an infirmary. None of the sisters was practicing nursing, though several still worked in the adjacent hospital.

Slender, gray-haired Sister Marion Chaloux recalled that she entered the convent at Colchester in 1940. "I remember at that time we had a farm here, chickens and pigs," she said. Sister Marion is the archivist of Religious Hospitalers at Colchester. She noted in 1999 that 30 years had passed since any new sisters had entered the convent. "Materialism has crept into people's lives," she said. "We were poor, we didn't miss material things. People today have heard of everything. They don't want to give things up. And there are other ways to serve." She was careful to note that the convent at Colchester has 22 associate members, including some married couples.

"I'm 72 and one of the younger ones," said Sister Rita Vallee, superior of the convent. "We volunteer at the hospital. We serve the poor of the community. We volunteer here at the adult day care center. More and more, those we help in the infirmary are our members."

Does it trouble the sisters that the convent at Colchester seems to be dying out? Sister Marion said, "The Lord has work for us to do in our lifetime. The call we receive is not a human call. If God wants this work to continue, He will call others. It may be lay people. We don't know. Hopefully we have passed on our reason for being so that the seeds have been planted. What we have done will continue in some other form."

The aging and shrinking of some religious orders in Vermont deeply troubles Bishop Angell. "I do worry about it," he said, "Who is going to do this work? We're going to have to hire lay people to do what the religious have done. Their devotion and dedication have been truly extraordinary." He added, "We live in a materialistic age that puts things before people. It is one of the tragedies of our time. In the silence, in the spirituality of the time I grew up in, you could almost hear the Lord calling you. There are so many things that call young people today. It is very difficult."

Angell proudly states that the Diocese of Burlington is the only American diocese in which a Carthusian monastery exists. It sits high on Mount Equinox, the highest of Vermont's Taconic Mountains, which rises steeply above the village of Manchester, in southwestern Vermont. The Carthusians are a cloistered order; the monks live their lives simply and sparsely, talking little and praying much. Bishop Angell pays yearly visits to the monastery.

He said, "There is a spirit of joy in their lives that is incredible." The monastery is, he said, "a powerhouse of prayer."

It was to this monastery that Bishop Marshall sometimes retreated to the contemplative life. Marshall well understood cloistered orders and so, in 1978, when the mother abbot of the Benedictine Abbaye Sainte Marie des Deux Montagnes, near Montreal, came to Vermont seeking a site for a new monastery, the bishop of Burlington was most welcoming. Several years previously, a man in the Canadian border town of Westfield, Gerard Lavallee, had offered 325 acres of land to the Diocese of Burlington. The offer went unaccepted and on September 28, 1978, Lavallee deeded the property to his brother and sister-in-law. That very day a representative of Bishop Marshall, seeking a location for a Benedictine monastery in northern Vermont, expressed an interest in the land. Lavallee contacted his brother and sister-in-law and they promptly agreed to donate the parcel to the Benedictines. In his book on the monastery's beginnings, Dom Guy-Marie Oury described the chosen location:

> The Benedictine monastery of nuns dedicated to the Immaculate Heart of Mary lies isolated in the valley of the Missisquoi River, far from the village upstream, Lowell, and from the village downstream, Westfield. In order not to disappoint the good Saint Benedict, the monastery was set on

Groundbreaking, Westfield Convent.

a ledge, high enough above the brook to look like a city built on a hill or a house built on a rock. The river has fits of madness as it enters from the south into the land of the nuns through an impressive little narrow gorge. Afterward, running northward in a series of large curves, the stream is much quieter, until the two cliffs open to let it go.

Construction of the monastery at Westfield began in 1980, just prior to the Feast of St. Benedict, on the 1,500th anniversary of the birth of the Benedictines' founder. Eight nuns arrived to take up residence in October of 1981. The place has thrived ever since; in 1990, a new wing was added. Fifteen sisters now dwell at the monastery, a walled brick structure with bell tower that commands a sweeping view of the border country and its highest summit, Jay Peak.

"Mass is the center of our life," according to Sister Laurence Couture, speaking in the fall of 1999 through the iron screen in the visitors room that separates the sisters from the outside world. She described a structured life of Mass, personal prayer, sacred readings, work, and singing. The sisters, she said, live in cells seven and a half feet wide by 12 feet, seven inches long. In each is a bed, two chairs, a kneeler, desk, and table. They seldom leave the monastery, but do go forth to visit doctor and dentist, and to vote. They have a goal of becoming financially self-sufficient and have begun making altar breads, which they sell far and wide. Their market is growing. They

Weston Priory.

also have a large vegetable garden and raise blueberries and strawberries. They enjoy two periods of recreation each day, and in wintertime toboggan and cross-country ski. The monastery welcomes visitors.

More than 100 miles to the south, also close by the main ridge of Vermont's Green Mountains, stands another Benedictine monastery. The Weston Priory, in its sylvan setting near the base of Terrible Mountain, is the most famous monastery in Vermont, its fame having spread through the music of its brothers. Recordings of their singing sell all through the English-speaking world. The fame of the priory peaked in the 1970's, when sometimes 1,000 people would attend Sunday Mass there. Despite it all, the monks at Weston have always described themselves as living by the work of their hands.

The priory was founded in 1953 by a Benedictine monk, Brother Leo Rudloff, a native of Germany, who had been abbot of the Dormition Abbey on Mount Zion in Israel. There, in the difficult days after World War II and the Holocaust, a group of German brothers living on the hill that, tradition holds, is the place where Mary died, had established a monastery as a place for dialogue to take place between Christians and Jews. In 1953, when Brother Leo came to the United States seeking to open a new monastery to support the Dormition Abbey and its work of reconciliation, he was warmly welcomed in Vermont by Bishop Ryan, ever determined to bring Catholicism to the rural areas. An old farm, surrounded by Green Mountain National Forest land, was purchased in the very rural south-central Vermont town of Weston. Work immediately began on renovating the old farmhouse and an adjacent henhouse. Most appropriately, the new monastery was welcomed to the Diocese of Burlington with ceremonies in the Queen City's South Park that included music by the Trapp Family Singers.

"Monks long ago went to the edge of the wilderness to live the Christian life. It has been so here," according to Brother John, a robust and bright-eyed septuagenarian who, in 1999, completed his 34th year at the priory. The monk, a native of Burlington whose father worked for Bishop Joyce, was for several years a priest in St. Johnsbury. Then he received permission from the bishop to enter the priory. "It was quite a change," he recalls of his transition from parish priest to manual laborer. In the early years he and his fellow monks lived in the converted henhouse, through the old cracked boards of which the winter winds often entered. But from the first, Brother John loved the Benedictine life. "We have long hours of prayer and of work. Ours is a life of prayer, work, and fraternal exchange," he said.

In the priory's early years, the brothers operated a dairy farm. "But after eight years of farming," Brother John recalled, "the cows were milking the community." Now the brothers run a tree farm, selling pulpwood, logs, and firewood. They also sell their pottery, graphics, weaving, copper, and silver work. And, of course, they sell recordings of their famous music. "Benedictines always sing their prayers," said Brother John. "The one who sings prays twice, St. Augustine said." The Weston Priory is self-supporting.

While the Benedictine sisters to the north at Westfield live a very cloistered life, mostly withdrawn from the world, the brothers at Weston have chosen at times to become very much involved in the secular world. Beginning in the 1960's, the brothers entered the civil rights movement, and some participated in Dr. Martin Luther King's Birmingham march. They have also been involved in the world peace and disarmament movements. In 1984, the brothers gave sanctuary to an Indian couple with five children from Guatemala. According to Brother John, the father was one of 17 catechists teaching reading to Indians in the mountains of Guatemala. The government took strong issue with their efforts, and the man who came with his family to the Green Mountains was the only one of the 17 to survive. "What are we about?" said Brother John. "We are about real reconciliation in the world. Sometimes you have to reach out to the world."

In Colchester are the Fathers and Brothers of St. Edmund, an order originally established in France, who teach at St. Michael's College and staff several Vermont parishes, including those at Swanton, Highgate and St. Anne's Shrine.

The Sisters of St. Joseph, a religious order also originating in France, began sending sisters to America in the 19th Century. In 1873, at the request of Bishop de Goesbriand and the pastor of St. Peter's Parish in Rutland, five

Edmundite Fathers.

nuns were sent to Rutland to establish a house and school, becoming an independent diocesan congregation in 1876.

The sisters went on to establish convents and schools in Bellows Falls, Fair Haven, Brattleboro, and Bennington, as well as doing catechetical work in many parishes and missions. They have been the backbone of Catholic education in southern Vermont for more than a century.

But not all religious orders in Vermont are represented by groups of the religious. In the woods above the northern Vermont village of Danville, in a cabin he built in 1967, lives Fr. Jon Bruder, a Trappist monk. A tall, gaunt, kindly man, Father Jon in the fall of 1999 was well into his eighth decade. He decided to make Vermont his home after wandering the country from coast to coast for weeks, in the mid-1960's, on a 90 day $99 bus ticket. "I found the place I was looking for," he said more than three decades after finding Danville. A self-described hermit who lives alone in his little cabin, without indoor plumbing, he is fond of saying, "I'm an independent cuss." Yet Father Jon has a remarkable number of friends throughout the country. The task each year of sending Christmas messages is for him a weeks-long undertaking.

Though he prefers the quiet of the woods and his small cabin to the loud and profit-driven outside world, once Jon Bruder saw the world at some of its worst. Just out of a Michigan high school in 1942, he enlisted in the air force and was trained as a navigator. He flew 50 combat missions out of southern Italy, guiding a big B-24 bomber to strike targets in Nazi-held Europe. Despite heavy anti-aircraft fire that time and again struck his plane, he came through the war without a scratch. On the advice of his brother, he became a priest, but found the life unsatisfying until he made the decision that "I want to be alone with God."

During his Vermont years, he has served as a fill-in priest in many parishes, conducted retreats, and, according to a neighbor, "has had the knack of showing up when people are in need." He said one chilly day in the last November of the millennium, seated in his warm cabin, "My life is being in God's presence and imploring Him to bless His world. I wish to be a channel for His peace and love."

Father Jon is a painter in oils, and a poet. He concluded a poem he wrote in 1984, titled "The Mystery of Love," as follows:

there is a love we hear of
but seldom touch and see
it is the source of life itself
in the heart of you and me . . .
it blooms the flower's petals

it melts the winter snow—
but none can bear to see it all
and only glimpses show
your eyes for me are windows
your heart is just a spark
a shadow of the whole
and each of us a part . . .
His love would overwhelm us
too much for us to see
so He gave me you—to remember Him
and for you—He gave you me.

Far away from Danville, over the hills and mountains in lakeside
Burlington, the fall sun moved to the rim of the Adirondacks as Bishop Angell
talked, in his diocesan office, of his Vermont years.

It is in the area of education that Angell sees some of the brightest hope.
"There is no substitute for Catholic schools," he said. "Two schools have
just opened. Two more will open next year, and one soon after that. People
want their children to have a disciplined education. We offer that. And the
numbers, the enrollment, in our schools is steadily on the increase. It is very
encouraging. I do worry about our Catholic schools becoming elitist. Education there is becoming so expensive. Some people can't afford a Catholic
education. We need to establish a scholarship fund. But the signs are good."

In Middlebury in 1941, parishioners of St. Mary's Church built, with
volunteer labor, a three-story brick building to house a grade school. It operated until 1971 when, refusing to charge tuition despite rising costs and a
shortage of teachers, the parishioners reluctantly decided to close. Gradually
the building deteriorated. Recently, however, nearly 100 parishioners turned
out to replaster walls and ceilings, saving the old building, where many of
them had attended school, from demolition. What was the motivation?

"It has always been our hope to have our school again," according to
Sally Foley, a Middlebury housewife and grandmother who has long been a
leader in the effort to bring Catholic education back to Addison County. "In
the fall we will open a K through four school, and within three or four years
it should be K through eight," she said. "When Father McDermott came
here four years ago he said, 'It would be wonderful to have a school.' That
was all we needed."

By the spring of 1999, teachers and a principal were hired for the
Middlebury school, and children were being enrolled. "We will have slightly
longer school days," said Foley, "and more school days than public schools.

We will be a very good school. We are determined to send our children into the world as better people, as better Catholic Christians. Who knows? We may get a nun or a priest out of this."

Beginning in 1962, the number of students enrolled in Catholic schools in Vermont steadily declined. But since 1991, those numbers have begun a slow but steady increase. In 1998, the school year opened with 3,334 students. "Four years ago, some parents began having conversations with us about schools," according to Sister Marianne Read, R.S.M., diocesan superintendent of schools. Speaking in the winter of 1999, she said, "They were interested in morals, respect, discipline, good academics. We said to them, 'You've got to prove your case.' Some didn't follow through, but others have. In September 1998, we opened Good Shepherd School in St. Johnsbury, K through eight, and Bishop John A. Marshall School in Morrisville, also K through eight. Schools are preparing to open in Middlebury and Springfield. The people of Morrisville hope to open a high school. The parents want morals and values taught to their kids. We are pushing for a scholarship line item in every Catholic school budget. The schools are the future for the church."

According to Bishop Angell, "Above all we must take care of the children. They are our hope. There is so much hope now in our schools, in the growing interest in a Catholic education." The bishop added that, in looking to the new millennium, "evangelization" is very high on his list of concerns:

He said, "We find that perhaps half of all Vermonters do not have any religious affiliation. I wonder, how do we get the message of the Lord to these people? That, it seems to me, is the big challenge of the millennium. We offer them, we can give them, a faith to live by. We can give them the good news that Christ died for them. When I was in Newport, in Rhode Island, I came to know the servants in those great houses, and I saw that to be a servant is a difficult way of life. You sit and wait for the people upstairs to ring the bell, and you have to be waiting and ready, at all times, ready to serve. A priest's life is like that. You have to put aside your golf game, put down your book. You have to be a servant to God's people. Christ said, 'I have not come to be served, but to serve.' We are here for the people. We offer what we have for everyone. The church is here to help people. We are here in Vermont, more than 100 churches and priests. We are here to serve. We have come a long way. But there is much, so much, that is left to be done."

Epilogue

THE NIGHT BEFORE THE CHRISTMAS—the millennium year of 2000 just seven days from being a single year away, near midnight, the faithful made their way through a chill Burlington night to old stone St. Joseph's Church (to become a co-cathedral in less than a year). Inside, the warmth, the candlelight, and the singing of a small choir were most welcoming. The mighty Hutchings organ, built for Chicago's Columbian Exposition in 1893, was played softly, only occasionally betraying its formidable power. Yet when its bass keys were touched, one wondered whether the deep sound may have shuddered the bones of Father Cloarec, deep beneath the altar. The great church, with its high barrel-vaulted ceiling and mighty fluted Romanesque columns, has been known to all the leaders of the Diocese of Burlington. The determined de Goesbriand said Mass there, as did builder Michaud, frail aesthetic Rice, tough Brady, fatherly Ryan, ecumenical Joyce, Marshall the quiet son of Rome, and the ever-outgoing Angell. The choir and congregation joined in the singing of "Silent Night, Holy Night," and a procession bearing tall flickering candles made its way into the sanctuary and to the altar, where gentle light touched the crèche and the little figures of Mary, Joseph, and the Christ Child in their fragile manger.

It was well past midnight when the service ended. Outside, the stars were seen brightly shining above Burlington. Historical origins beckoned; the route was to the north, through the streets of the quiet city and on into the darkness of the snow-covered Champlain Valley countryside. The road angled north, then west, into the islands of Lake Champlain, to Isle La Motte and, somewhere near 1:30 a.m., to St. Anne's Shrine. All was calm by the cold dark lake. Only the stars were bright, and a few lights on the New York shore. Among the sheltering cedars, the Stations of the Cross could dimly be seen, supported by piles of rock from the foundation of the French fort built in 1666. The stations stand within the confines of the fort, where nearly three-and-a-third centuries before was built the little chapel where Mass was first said on land that would one day be part of the state of Vermont. To be there in the darkness of that early Christmas morning was to gain some understanding of the vast isolation and loneliness those Europeans must have felt in an uncharted place so strange and far from home. Then an icy wind stirred the cedars, an acute reminder of the frontier's harshness for those who came in little boats and struggled for warmth in their wooden outpost. Through the trees could be seen a halo of light, crowning an imposing gilded statue of the Virgin Mary. Once it shone atop the tallest tower of the old cathedral at Burlington, standing watch over the city by the inland sea. Placed there by Bishop Michaud on his return from Lourdes, the first light of a winter morning in 1972 showed that it had miraculously survived the conflagration almost unscathed. In the warm months of the coming summer, the faithful, by the thousands, would return to Isle La Motte and the Shrine of St. Anne. But on this dark, early Christmas morning only the stars were there, the cold wind, the statue beneath its crown of light, and the ever-present sense of history.

Driving homeward, one saw the night lights of farmhouses gleaming out in the old farm fields of the islands, while streetlights dimly lit the little villages. Soon Burlington cast a broad glow upon the sky, and that glow became a multitude of lights as the swift highway led through the sprawling, darkened city. Moving down the great highway, one saw the Green Mountains looming darkly to the east, their snowy crests just visible against the now-clouded sky. Here and there the darkness was broken by the colored lights of Christmas, some surely burning to welcome late travelers home for the holiday. The way led far down the state onto narrow two-lane roads among the hills. Here and there in the night were seen the houses of worship of the Catholic faith, from the modest wooden structures of the country hamlets to the towering brick-and-stone structures of the towns. Before the sun rose through a haze of morning clouds, the rim of the ancient mountains was set in bold relief against the golden light of a Christmas morning. When the first beams touched the eastern hilltops, their icy crests reflected the reds and golds of dawn's first rays, the beginning of a beautiful winter day in Vermont. The previous autumn the eighth bishop of Burlington, Kenneth Angell, had been in the presence of the Holy Father in Rome and had asked him to recall his time in Vermont. Pope John Paul II paused, searching his memory for those few brief days before he was called to his demanding tasks as the spiritual leader of the world's Catholics. He had been a much younger man when he walked the hills above the White River, pitched hay, swam in a chill upland pond, and said Mass while the people and the animals of a Pomfret farm looked on. Now the years and a would-be assassin's bullet had taken a mighty toll. The Holy Father turned his thoughts back past more than two momentous decades and smiled when he said to the bishop of Burlington, "Vermont, yes Vermont. How beautiful was Vermont."

Sources

Ballway, Eleanor W., editor. *Fairfield, Vermont Reminiscences.*. Fairfield Bicentennial Committee. Essex Publishing Company, 1977.

Blow, David J. "The Catholic Parochial Schools of Burlington, *1853–1918.*" *Proceedings of the Vermont Historical Society,* Vol. 54, No. 3, Summer 1976.
———. *A History of the Holy Rosary Parish, Richmond, Vermont,* 1972.

Book Committee of Holy Angels Parish. *A History of Holy Guardian Angels Parish, 1872–1997.* L. G. Printing, St. Albans, Vermont, 1997.

Cadden, John J. *Father Jeremiah O'Callaghan: Economist and Pioneer Missionary.* Thesis for M.A. at Catholic University. Washington, D. C., 1936.

Centennial History: St. Anthony's, White River Junction, Vermont. St. Anthony's Parish, White River Junction, Vermont, 1969.

Conley, Patrick T. *Catholicism in Rhode Island: The Formative Era.* The Diocese of Providence, Rhode Island, 1976.

Coolidge, Guy O. *The French Occupation of the Champlain Valley.* Vermont Historical Society, September 1938.

Couture, Rev. Joseph N. *The Catholic Clergy of Vermont, 1964.* Unpublished.

Croteau, Colette. *History of the Parish of St. Rose of Lima.* Free Press Printing Company, Burlington, Vermont, 1946.

Davis, Robert S. "A Leap into History: Vermonter Recalls Valor of Normandy Troopers." *The Sunday Times Argus,* Barre, Vermont, 5 June, 1994.

de Goesbriand, Louis. *Catholic Memoirs of Vermont and New Hampshire.* Burlington, Vermont, 1886.

———— *The Labors of the Apostles.* Benziger Brothers, New York, Cincinnati, and Chicago, 1893.

Durick, Jeremiah K. *The Catholic Church in Vermont: A Centennary History.* Roman Catholic Diocese of Burlington, Burlington, Vermont, 1953.

Ferland, *Suszanne F.* "How Three Community Hospitals Came to Be." *Hall A.,* a publication of the Medical Center Hospital of Vermont, Fall 1997.

Hannon, Rev. Patrick T. *Immaculate Conception of Mary Parish.* Immaculate Conception of Mary Parish, St. Albans, Vermont, 1977.

Haskins, Harold W. *A History of Bradford, Vermont.* Littleton, New Hampshire, 1968.

Healy, Michael J. *Walking in the Spirit: Fanny Allen Hospital, 1884–1894.* Fanny Allen Hospital, Colchester, Vermont, 1993.

Hill, Ralph N. *Lake Champlain: Key to Liberty.* The Countryman Press, Woodstock, Vermont, 1976.

History of St. Thomas's Church, Underhill Center, Vermont. St. Thomas's Church, 1991.

History of St. Peter Parish. St. Peter Parish, Rutland, Vermont, 1979.

Holmes, David R. *Stalking the Academic Communist: Intellectual Freedom and the Firing of Alex Novikoff.* The University Press of New England, Burlington, Vermont, 1989.

Jennings, Lt. David. Korean War letters. Special Collections, Bailey/Howe Library, University of Vermont, Burlington, Vermont.

Joyce, Robert F. Oral history, interviewed by Dr. Paul French, December 1969. Special Collections, Bailey/Howe Library, University of Vermont, Burlington, Vermont, 1969.

Joyce, Robert F. *Thoughts to Ponder.* The Daughters of St. Paul, Boston, Massachusetts, 1980.

Kaufman, Martin. *University of Vermont College of Medicine.* University of Vermont College of Medicine and University Press of New England, Hanover, New Hampshire, 1979.

Kerlidou, Rev. Joseph M.; Rev. Joseph N. Couture; and Rev. Maurice U. Boucher. *St. Anne's Shrine.* Regal Art Press, St. Albans, Vermont, 1979.

Mahoney, Rev. John P. Reports and letters to the diocese from the South Pacific 1942–1945. Diocesan archive.

Maurice, Maggie. *"A Man of Peace." Burlington Free Press.* 1 Sept. , 1985.

Neal, Maudean. *Firey Crosses in the Green Mountains.* Greenhills Books, Randolph, Vermont, 1989.

Nolin, Sister Margaret. *History of Bishop De Goesbriand Hospital 1924– 1967, As I Remember It.* Unpublished. Diocesan archive.

Novikoff, Dr. Alex. Transcript of interview at the University of Vermont, 23 May, 1983. Special Collections, Bailey/Howe Library, University of Vermont, Burlington, Vermont.

Patrick, Michael; Evenly, Sheets; and Evelyn, Trickel. *The Story of the Orphan Trains.* The Lightning Tree Press, Santa Fe, New Mexico, 1990.

Popecki, Joseph T. *The Parish of St. Mark's in Burlington, Vermont, 1941– 1991.* Queen City Printers, Burlington, Vermont, 1991.

Roth, Stephen. *A History of Trinity College,* Trinity College, Burlington, Vermont, 1975.

Saint Mary Star of the Sea 1873–1973. The Parish History Committee, Newport, Vermont, 1973.

Saint Stanislaus Kostka, West Rutland, Vermont, 1904–1989. St. Stanislaus Kostka, 1989.

Vermont Catholic Tribune. 1956 to present. Diocesan archive.

INDEX

C

Camp Holy Cross, 90
Candon, Elizabeth, 150–51
Carmelite Sisters, 93
Caron, Joan, 166
Caron, Paul, 110
Carthusian Fathers, 93, 168–69
Carthusian Monastery, 148, 168–69
Carty, Thomas, 40
Cathedral High School, 55
Cathedral of the Immaculate Conception, 28, 146, 147–48
Catholic Church
    beginnings of, in Vermont, vii, 5–6
    growth of, in Vermont, 15, 16–17
    liberalization of, 129–37
    priest shortage and, 163–64
Catholic Daughters of America, 62
Catholic Rural Life Institute, 90–91
Catholic schools
    under Bishop Angell, 174–75
    under Bishop de Goesbriand, 25, 27
    under Bishop Rice, 54–56
    enrollment in, under Bishop Joyce, 137–39
    first Vermont, 17
    importance of, 137
Catholics
    French-Canadian, 30–31, 48
    growing ethnic diversity of, 40–41
    increasing population of, in Vermont, 39, 40
    Irish, 6, 10, 14–15, 16–17, 30–31
    Italian, 41
    Polish, 40–41
Chaloux, Gerard, 113
Chaloux, Marion, 168
Champlain, Samuel de, vii, 2–3
Chenette, Donalda, 116, 138
Cheney, Patricia, 118, 119
churches
    constructed under Bishop de Goesbriand, 18–19, 21–25
    constructed under Bishop Michaud, 41–43
    constructed under Bishop Rice, 62, 98
    constructed under Bishop Ryan, 92–95
    early Vermont, 10–11, 18
    Holy Guardian Angels Church, 25
    Middlebury Church, 8
    Our Lady Star of the Sea, 33
    Sacre Couer de Marie Church, 42

on Bishop Ryan, 87, 93
condolences for Jacqueline Kennedy of, 132
Gibson, Ernest, 97
Gillis, Joseph, 45, 53
Gokey, Francis X., 145
Golden, Karen, 136
Great Depression, 65
Guare, Paul, 108
Gyra, Frank, 114, 129

H
Hemenway, Abby Maria, 26
Hendy, Elias, 41, 58
Heon, Gerald, 112, 114
Highter, Jean, 111, 136
Hill, Ralph Nading, 3
Holy Guardian Angels Church, 25
Holy Rosary Parish, 65
Hoover, Herbert, 64–65
hospitals, 34–35, 59–62, 139, 152
Houde, Paul, 115, 116
House of Discernment, 163–64
Houthakker, Anna-Teresa, 1, 2
Houthakker, Hendrik, 1, 2
Hunt, Joe, 80–81
Hurley, Ed, 136
Hyde, Archibald, 7

I
influenza epidemic, 57–58
Irish Catholics, unrest between French-Canadians and, 30–31, 48
Irish immigrants, 6, 10, 14–15, 16–17
Italian Catholics, 41

J
Jennings, David, 99, 100–3
Jesuit missionaries, 3–4
Jogues, Isaac, St., 4
John Paul II, 143–44, 151, 177. *See also* Wojtyla, Karol
John XXIII, 129
Johnson, Joseph, 121
Joyce, Robert F.
    on abortion, 139–40
    Alex Novikoff and, 124–26
    appointed Bishop of Burlington, 120–21, 126
    as Bishop of Burlington, 126–42
    Burlington hospitals and, 139
    Catholic schools and, 137–39
    early life of, 121–23
    liberalization of the Church and, 129–37

as priest, 123–24
retirement of, 140–42
at Vatican II, 129–34

K

Kalm, Peter, 4
Kearney, Edward, 39–40
Keeley, Patrick Charles, 19, 161
Kelly, Michael, 34
Kennedy, John F., 132, 159–60
Kennedy, John M., 103
Kolozdiej, Francis, 41
Korean War, 100–4
Ku Klux Klan, 63–64

L

labor movement, 76–80
Laroche, Leonidas, 116, 117
Law, Bernard, 1, 155
Limoge, Jack, 64
Lincoln, Abraham, 21
Loeb, William, 76–77
Lonergan, John, 19, 20–21, 21–22
Loretto Home, 37

M

Mahoney, John P., 78, 80–84
Major, Norma, 118
Major, Paul, 118, 119
Markey, Edward, 115
Marshall, Ann, 109, 119
Marshall, John A.
    appointed Bishop of Burlington, 144–47
    on Bishop Joyce, 127
    as Bishop of Burlington, 147–54
    early life of, 147
    leaves Vermont, 153–55
    on political issues, 150–51
    study of American seminaries by, 151–53
    Vatican II and, 148
Martino, Dorothy, 111
Martocci, Frank, 112
Matignon, François, 6
Matthew, St., vii
Maurice, Maggie, 140–41
Mayo, Reid, 108, 137
McClintock, Mary, 40, 148–49, 151, 152, 155
McCready, William, 63–64
McGovney, John, 68
McKeough, Mary, 61, 62

McSweeney, John, 114, 143, 147, 152–53, 154
McVinney, Russell, 160
Mercure, Jeannine, 166
Michaud, John S.
 as Bishop of Burlington, 34–47
 as coadjutor of Burlington Diocese, 31
 construction by, 27, 33, 36–38, 41–43
 early life of, 31–33
 health problems of, 32, 35–36, 45, 46
 later years of, 45–47
 St. Joseph's Providence Orphan Asylum and, 27, 33
 as young priest, 33–34
Michulka, Valentine, 40, 41
Middlebury Church, 8
Mignault, Pierre Marie, 5, 6
Miller, Walter, 147, 164
Monahan, Mary, 60
monasteries, 168–72
Morency, Rita, 114
Moyers, William, 63–64
Moynihan, Helen, 111, 112
N
Naramore, Vincent, 64, 74–75, 93, 98, 107, 135
National War Labor Board, 78–79
Newport affair, 43–44, 53
Nolin, Margaret, 60–62
Novikoff, Alex, 124–26
O
O'Callaghan, Jeremiah
 arrival in Vermont of, 6–7
 baptismal record of, 10
 Bishop Angell on, vii
 in later years, 11–12
 missionary work of, 8–9, 11–12
 sermons of, 8–9
 St. Mary's Church and, 7–8
 writings of, 11
Omland, Carolyn, 108, 109
orphan trains, 39
orphanages, 17, 25, 27–28, 33
O'Sullivan, Daniel, 45–46, 48
O'Sullivan, Thomas, 48
Our Lady Star of the Sea, 33
Oury, Guy-Marie, 169–70
P
Parmenter, George, 111, 112
parochial schools. *See* Catholic schools

T

Tennien, William
  labor movement and, 76–77, 79
  St. Mark's Church and, 75–76
Thoughts to Ponder (Joyce), 127
Tilden, Joseph, 109
Towne, Charles, 51
Trinity College, 55–56, 70

V

Vallee, Rita, 168
Vatican II, 129–34, 148
Vermont
  beginnings of Catholic Church in, vii, 5–6
  growth of Catholic Church in, 15, 16–17
  homefront during World War II, 75–80
  increasing Catholic population in, 39, 40
  Irish immigration to, 6, 10
  labor movement, 76–80
  Protestants in, 15
  during Revolutionary War, 4–5
Vermont Catholic Charities, 70
Verret, John J., 72–74
Vietnam War, 137, 150, 151
Villeneuve, Phil, 114

W

Wells, Gordon, 63–64
Weston Priory, 171–72
Wheeler, John, 10
White, Eugene, 63–64
Wojtyla, Karol, 1–2, 143–44. *See also* John Paul II
World War I, 56–57
World War II
  army chaplains during, 71–75
  correspondence between Bishop Brady and father Mahoney during, 80–84
  Vermont homefront during, 75–80

Y

Young, Geraldine, 108

Z

Ziter, Ella, 113